NIGHT LIGHT

NIGHT LIGHT

A BOOK OF NIGHTTIME MEDITATIONS

Amy E. Dean

HAZELDEN

Hazelden
Center City, Minnesota 55012-0176

ISBN-13: 978-0-89486-381-3
ISBN-10: 0-89486-381-9

You do build in darkness if you have faith. When the light returns you have made of yourself a fortress which is impregnable to certain kinds of trouble; you may even find yourself needed and sought by others as a beacon in their dark.

—*Olga Rosmanith*

INTRODUCTION

When I entered the program in May 1983, I suddenly discovered I had incredible feelings I had never allowed myself to feel. Those feelings were fear, anxiety, and loneliness. For years I had built up walls and defenses that repelled those feelings, but the program took away my defenses.

I found those negative feelings particularly prevalent at night. I would be fine all day and even at an evening meeting. But after the meeting I would come home and have overwhelming feelings of loneliness and fear. Sometimes I had a difficult time getting to sleep. Sometimes I would wake up in the middle of the night and stay up for hours with anxious feelings. What was it about the nighttime that was so difficult?

I soon discovered daylight chased away many of my fears because of the hustle-bustle of the day. There were things to do, people to see, and—as Robert Frost says—"miles to go before I sleep." Each new dawn held new promises and new beginnings. But what did the sunset hold? What was there to focus on at night? The meditations on the following pages are designed to help keep your program in focus at night. Each meditation focuses on a particular issue or feeling you may feel at the end of the day. The meditation then provides you with program tools to ease your mind gently into a relaxed state at bedtime.

It's so true that the program works, but only if you work it. None of us can get better without the help of the Twelve Steps, sponsors, slogans, the fellowship, our Higher Power, prayer, and meditation. Each of these nightly meditations reminds you of the marvelous tools you have available and helps you keep them ever-present. With them, you are truly never alone, no matter what time of day ... or night.

—Amy E. Dean

JANUARY

It is as important to relax our minds as it is to concentrate them.
—*Charles B. Newcomb*

After a day of activity, our bodies naturally need to slow down. We yawn, our muscles stiffen, our eyes want to close. Yet our minds can be racing at top speed. How do we learn to slow down our thoughts and relax? We first need to realize we don't have to do it all ourselves. We can ask for help from a book, a relaxation tape, a class or workshop, a movie, or music. And we can learn how to unwind from others.

For most of our lives, we learned how to be tense. Now we need to learn how to relax. Just as we didn't learn our tension in one night, we also won't learn relaxation in one night. But we can begin tonight to find some methods that will work for us. We can try, a little bit at a time, to become familiar with how it feels to have a more relaxed mind. Tonight can be a beginning.

Am I willing to unlearn my tensions? What resources can I use tonight to help me relax my mind?

But where was I to start? The world is so vast, I shall start with the country I knew best, my own. But my country is so very large. I had better start with my town. But my town, too, is large. I had best start with my street. No, my home. No, my family. Never mind, I shall start with myself.
—Elie Wiesel

How many times have we tried to change things outside of ourselves, like a parent, a loved one, a drinking or drug-using pattern, or a boss? Perhaps we felt if we changed someone or something, we would be better off. But we soon discovered we were powerless to change people, places, or things.

All we can change is ourselves. Yet we can't do that by five-minute overhauls. Nor can we go to bed at night and expect to wake up the next day as the person we always wanted to be.

We need to *keep it simple* as we change ourselves. We need to start slowly. If we imagine ourselves as a big puzzle with many pieces, we may understand we can only see our whole selves by joining together one piece at a time.

Did I try to change others today? How can I keep it simple as I try to change myself—just a little bit at a time?

Strange feelings. . . . Just a sort of unexplained sadness that comes each afternoon when the new day is gone forever and there's nothing ahead but increasing darkness.
—*Robert M. Pirsig*

Just as each day is a new beginning, so is each night also a new start. Each night can be a chance to recharge ourselves after our day's batteries have run down. Each night can be a chance to start anew on our goals, our growth, our good thoughts.

Instead of reflecting on the past events of the day, we can look forward to the moments to come. We can be unafraid of the darkness of the night as we prepare for tomorrow by using positive energy.

Although the day is done, tomorrow is yet to come. There are plans to make, places to go, people to see, and projects to do. Tomorrow can begin with hope and strength and energy directed to all our forthcoming events.

I can see tomorrow as a new beginning.

Happiness is not pleasure. Happiness is victory.
—*Zig Ziglar*

Many people believe happiness is measured in material terms: a house, money, lots of clothes. Others believe it's found in enjoyable moments: a sunset, dinner with friends, a walk in the woods. Although happiness is all these things, it's also the feeling we get when we have achieved something we've longed for and worked hard for. Happiness can be a personal victory.

To be victorious doesn't mean we have to win. It can mean we've gone beyond an expected outcome and gained more than we hoped for. There have been times when we've experienced victory: passing a test, buying our first car, graduating from college, landing a job, living on our own. But all victories don't have to be big. They can be as small and insignificant as losing a few pounds, going a few hours without a drink or other drug, not arguing with a family member, or taking an hour for ourselves.

Big or small, our victories are our happiness. Each one shows us we can do what we set out to do. Each helps build confidence in our abilities and is a boon to our self-esteem. With each victory, we can be assured there will be another.

I can be happy for all my victories.

You will forget your misery; you will remember it as waters that have passed away.

—Job 11:16

Many of us have painful memories we carry with us like pictures in a wallet. We keep these memories alive through feelings generated by those moments. Why are we so attached to unpleasant memories?

It's difficult to let go of memories, no matter how unpleasant. Sometimes they're a reminder of the past, but more often we clutch them because we're afraid to feel pleasant feelings today. Because the program is working in our lives, we have fewer painful times now. That may not be comfortable, so we invent new pain or dredge up the sludge of the past. As ugly as it may be, it's still familiar.

Tonight we don't have to look back. We don't have to feel misery or pain because it's familiar. We don't have to drag out that wallet and look at the images of unhappy times again. Tonight we can leave those spaces in our wallets empty, ready to be filled with new moments to remember.

I can try to make some new moments to remember. I don't need to look back anymore.

So every faithful heart shall pray to Thee in the hour of anxiety, when great floods threaten. Thou art a refuge to me from distress so that it cannot touch me; Thou dost guard me in salvation beyond all reach of harm.

—Psalm 32

It's difficult to focus on the present when our minds are thinking of events yet to come. We may be so obsessed with an upcoming happening that we forget to stay in the present.

Perhaps we've been asked to speak at a meeting. Or maybe we have a big test tomorrow. Or maybe we have some plans days from now for a party, a family get-together, or a trip, that are already sending us into a whirlwind of tension and anxiety.

To stay in the present, we need to ask for help. Our Higher Power can help us with our anxiety about a future event, whether the event will happen five minutes, five days, or five years from now. Tonight and tomorrow will happen, no matter how much anxiety we have. But future events may turn out a little better if we take some serenity from our Higher Power with us.

Is an upcoming event causing me a lot of anxiety? How can I use the program to help me let go of this anxiety?

Prayer should be the key of the day and the lock of the night.

—Old proverb

Many of us believe prayer has to be scheduled—a once-in-the-morning and once-at-night routine. Yet few of us remember prayer is merely a conversation with our Higher Power. We can pray anytime and as often as we'd like.

Prayer in the morning is a wonderful way to open the day. Yet do we continue to keep the door open by renewing our conversation with our Higher Power? Do we turn to our Higher Power during times of stress, joy, sadness, or peace? We may be so busy in our daily tasks that we forget to keep that door open.

Tonight the door is still open. Our Higher Power is still there to listen. We can share our feelings of the day as though we were talking to a close friend. We don't have to prostrate ourselves before our Higher Power. All we have to do is start talking. Then we can close the door with prayer, knowing we have with us the good, warm feelings that faith brings. And as we finally lay down to sleep tonight, we can say good-night to our Higher Power and give thanks for the day.

Now I lay me down to sleep, I pray the Lord my soul to keep.

*Don't be afraid to take a big step. You can't cross
a chasm in two small jumps.*
—David Lloyd George

Taking a risk can be scary. Whether the risk involves a new relationship, asking for a raise, being
honest, or changing a behavior, it's still pretty hard to
do. Sometimes we may wish we could approach a risk
with only partial involvement, almost as if we had one
foot inside a door and one outside. That way, if things
get too difficult, we can always run away.

But we can't take a risk unless we commit ourselves
to it. And we can't commit ourselves unless we have
faith that no matter what happens, we're okay. We
may feel vulnerable, but we don't have to feel alone if
we remember our Higher Power is with us.

Perhaps we took a risk today and are still feeling
scared and exposed. Or maybe we're planning on taking a risk tomorrow and are filled with fear. Remember it's okay to have feelings of fear, doubt, and
insecurity.

*Tonight I will relax and know I never approach a risk
without my Higher Power to guide me.*

*Later. I'm still young. I'll think of spiritual things
when I'm older. On my deathbed.*
— *Garrison Keillor*

Too often we've thought prayer is for the aged, the
sick, or the dying. If we are young, healthy, and successful, we may think we don't need to communicate
with a Higher Power. "I'm fine right now," we may say.
"I will . . . later on."

The time to establish contact with a Higher Power is
now. From the minute we come kicking and screaming into this world until our last breath, there is a
Power greater than ourselves watching over us. This
Power guides us, strengthens us, and helps us grow
even without our acknowledging it is there. But it is
because we don't acknowledge its presence that we
become lost, confused, depressed, angry, hopeless, or
unforgiving.

Our time to reach out to our Higher Power is not
when our bodies stop running. Now is the time to ask
for direction, seek knowledge, become open to receiving divine guidance. If we open ourselves now to developing our spirituality, we will open a valuable door
to our growth.

---

*Can I begin to develop my spiritual beliefs? Can I open my
mind and heart to a Higher Power?*

Great Spirit, help me never to judge another until I have walked in his moccasins for two weeks.

—*Sioux Indian prayer*

How many times do we see someone who dresses or acts differently? How do we usually react to such a person? Do we stare or make a comment to someone next to us? Meetings are excellent places to come in contact with those who come from different backgrounds. Do we greet each person we meet with care and attention, or do we pass judgments and make jokes?

Our Higher Power has given each of us a diverse background and personality. Some of us have known incredible hardship or handicap. Some of us have limited education. Some of us live in crowded spaces. But some of us have had opportunities. Some of us have an educational degree. Some of us live in large homes. Yet is there any one of us who is better than another?

If we are prone to judge or criticize, tonight we can decide to take a first step toward silence. Remember that education and economics do not make someone better. We are the same, no matter how much, or how little, we have.

I can learn not to judge others.

Example is not the main thing in influencing others. It is the only thing.

—*Albert Schweitzer*

Imagine how useless meetings would be without examples of how well the program works. There would be no one who was clean and no one with the strength to cope with another's problem. Surely we could use the Steps and principles ourselves, but we'd feel lost and alone without the positive influences of others.

All around us are people who succeed in the program. Their strength and positive energy, their kind words and understanding nature, and their no-nonsense approach to living with faith and perseverance are an inspiration. The fact that they have changed for the better is the best illustration of how we can change.

Ask old-timers what they were like when they first came into the program. They'll say they were unhappy, confused, and near despair. But in the program they met others who had been there, too. It won't take us long to replace our frowns with smiles, our tension with relaxation, our anger with forgiveness. If we look to the examples around us, we will find strength.

Help me remember where I came from, and help me be grateful for how the program has guided me.

The first thing I had to conquer was fear. I realized what a debilitating thing fear is. It can render you absolutely helpless. I know now that fear breeds fear.

—Byron Janis

The future can be scary, especially if we try to predict what will happen. Sometimes we may even go further, not only predicting what may happen but also anticipating our reactions to those events. If only we knew what will happen, then we wouldn't have to be afraid of the future.

If we're not careful, we will allow every fearful feeling to overtake us until the fear extends into other parts of our lives. Fear can be like a hidden trap, catching us whenever we try to go anywhere or do anything. We cannot see, hear, or touch fear, but we can give it so much power that it almost has a life of its own.

We can get rid of the traps fear has set for us. We can do that by having faith in our Higher Power. We can have faith that our way has been prepared for us, faith that we are safe wherever we are.

I can cut the ties with which fear binds me. Without fear, I will only feel the safety of faith.

When health is absent, wisdom cannot reveal itself, art cannot manifest, strength cannot fight, wealth becomes useless, and intelligence cannot be applied.

—Herophilus

If we have ceased an obsessive behavior, we may think we are now healthy. Yet we may not be paying enough attention to our needs for sleep, good food, and exercise. We may also be ignoring our spiritual and mental health needs by not taking time to meditate or communicate with others.

Taking away an obsession doesn't mean we're cured. Instead, the work is just beginning. Now is the time to structure our days and nights to include time to be alone, time to listen to ourselves, and time to listen and talk with others.

We are now in the process of rebuilding ourselves into better people. We need to work on our outer appearances and our inner healthiness. Good nutrition, plenty of rest, a balance of exercise and play, meditation time, and a balance between work hours and home hours is needed for our best health. We can take the first healthy step toward building a better self.

Higher Power, help me look at my health. Can I identify areas that need improvement?

The doors we open and close each day decide the lives we live.

—*Flora Whittemore*

We often hear the phrase, "When one door shuts, another opens." It means everything has a beginning and an end. When our travels on one path are completed, another path lies ahead.

It's not easy to feel a door close. Relationships, friendships, careers, and lives end. Although we may not understand why a door closes, it's important to remember our Higher Power has everything to do with it. By the same token, we may not understand why certain doors open, revealing opportunities we may have longed for. Again, our Higher Power feels we are ready to pursue that new experience.

The doors that opened and closed today helped prepare us for our experiences tonight. The doors that opened and closed tonight will help us grow toward tomorrow. We are not mice in a maze, randomly pursuing paths for a reward of cheese. We are children of our Higher Power, guided towards our chosen goal through the many doors we open and close along the way.

Have I learned there is a reason for everything in my life? Can I trust that my path has been prepared for me by my Higher Power?

What was completely forbidden for me to do would be to kill myself. . . . If I were to commit suicide, I would be throwing God's gift back in his face.

—Dr. Raymond A. Moody

Many of us have had suicidal thoughts at one time or another. We hear at meetings how others have tried suicide in the past. We may have tried it ourselves or our lives may have been touched by the suicide of someone we knew. We may now find that living a clean, sober, spiritual life is overwhelming. Sometimes we may feel like giving up.

That's when we need to call someone. Talk it out. Or get to a meeting and be honest with the group about our feelings. There are people who care. Our friends and our peers are God's human messengers, ready to give understanding to those in need.

If a friend of ours felt down on life, wouldn't we want to help? Now is the time to open ourselves up to caring and love from another human being.

Do I think about giving up? Who can I open up to for caring and love?

*Let everyone sweep in front of his [or her] own
door, and the whole world will be clean.*
                                                —*Goethe*

Taking care of ourselves rather than trying to control others may be difficult. Our character defects may lead us to believe we should take responsibility for the actions of others. Sometimes we may feel we know how a spouse, co-worker, or friend should act. We may even go so far as to tell someone what he or she should do or do it for them.

Tonight we can reflect on our actions of today. Did we cover up another's behavior, or tell someone what to do, or take control of something that was not our responsibility? We need to realize that taking charge of another's life is not beneficial to anyone. Focusing on another's life keeps us from looking at ours. Doing for others what they should be doing for themselves takes away valuable lessons for growth.

What would happen if everyone in a classroom were the teacher? Who would listen and learn? Who would mature and grow? The teacher in our lives is our Higher Power. Let us respect our instructor and let our Higher Power do the guiding while we grow.

Help me listen and learn and let go of controlling others.

Enthusiasm is the yeast that makes your hopes rise to the stars. Enthusiasm is the sparkle in your eyes, the swing in your gait, the grip of your hand, the irresistible surge of will and energy to execute your ideas.

—Henry Ford

The automobile is just one of many inventions based on someone's enthusiasm to realize a dream. From the persistence came a machine that has since improved our lives by bringing people closer together.

Enthusiasm is a catalyst for improvement. If we think back to those times when we've felt enthusiasm in our lives, we'll realize its benefits. Perhaps we secured a job promotion or pitched a no-hitter or completed an intricate quilt.

Enthusiasm in the program is also a catalyst for change. If we observe those who truly work their program with passion, we'll see them making positive changes, gathering a greater sense of self-esteem. Their enthusiasm can be contagious if we open up our minds to their belief that all things are possible.

Have I been enthusiastic today? Can I learn from the enthusiasm of someone close to me?

Children do not know how their parents love them, and they never will till the grave closes over those parents, or till they have children of their own.

—Edmund Vance Cooke

As adults, we may feel we were cheated out of a "normal" childhood because of our parents' emotional, physical, or spiritual failings. We may think they should never be forgiven for their actions or inactions when we were young.

Yet imagine what our lives would be like today if we did not forgive. We would be bitter, stomping angrily through life with a clipboard in hand, ready to write down the name of the next person who crosses us. It's time to throw away the clipboard and the names on it—including the names of our parents.

The program teaches us to love those who come into our lives, even if we don't like them. It teaches us forgiveness through our Higher Power. We do not have to like our parents, but we can love them. By the same token, we need to realize our parents love us in their special way. They aren't perfect—and neither are we.

Help me remember my parents did the best they could with what they had. That's all anyone can really do.

And if not now, when?

—*The Talmud*

It's so easy to put things off. Sometimes we're like Scarlet O'Hara, who hoped and dreamed for a better life by saying, "There's always tomorrow." But is there always a tomorrow? If we live too many of our days counting on tomorrows, we may find ourselves putting off achievements and growth now.

What if tomorrow never came? What if all of our time to do what we wanted was put in the hours left in today? We'd be scurrying around like mice trying to cram as much as we could into this short period of time. But today, not having such a deadline, we believe our time is endless and no goal or task is so important that it can't be put off.

The time to achieve is now. The time to live is now. For as long as we believe tomorrow will come, we'll be living for tomorrow. If we don't believe today is the greatest gift we could receive, we'll never know how to live for today. Everything we want to achieve, to learn, to share can begin today. If we don't live the best we can right now, then when?

Higher Power, help me learn to use my time wisely. Help me avoid putting things off.

I came to understand that it was all right to do things for people as long as I did it for the sake of doing it . . . the value being more in the act than in the result.

—Joanna Field

We've all heard the sentiment that it is better to give than to receive. Yet we may find it difficult to give to others, whether that giving involves an actual gift or an act of giving of ourselves: caring for someone who is ill, running an errand for someone, giving a back-rub, or extending an invitation to someone who is alone.

We may feel afraid to do for others without any expectations of receiving something in return. To give unselfishly exposes our feelings and shows we care. Yet if we can look beyond our fears to the selflessness of our giving actions, there is a great reward: knowing we had the courage to risk giving to someone.

The risks we take in giving to others are lessons for ourselves as well as for those whose lives we touch. The gift of giving opens doors to the homes of our souls.

Did I take time today to give to others? Can I risk giving to someone close to me?

I am bigger than anything that can happen to me. All these things, sorrow, misfortune, and suffering are outside my door. I am in the house and I have the key.
—*Charles Fletcher Lummis*

So many things seem to loom over us. There's our addiction to alcohol or other drugs, food, or people. There are our fears of expressing love, of feeling, of being alone, of being abandoned, of being rejected, of failing. There are the miseries of childhood, unhappy relationships, a failed marriage, or death. Sometimes there's even the world in general—all people, places, and things. Some days just about everything seems ready to swallow us up.

Yet nothing has absolute power over us if we have a strong belief in ourselves and a Higher Power. Our Higher Power strengthens us and helps us stay in good condition.

The negative conditions we see are not lurking in the shadows, ready to spring upon us at any moment. There are not people "out to get us," nor traps set to foil our goals. We are secure because of the faith we have in our Higher Power.

The only thing in this life bigger than me is my Higher Power. Tonight I can feel safe and secure no matter where I am.

Be yourself. Who else is better qualified?
                                        —*Frank J. Giblin, II*

Almost every magazine devotes its cover to movie stars and famous personalities. We are taught that we need to look like the most attractive and glamorous people. We need to wear what they wear, eat what they eat, and fix our hair like theirs. The message we are given is: Don't be yourself, be like someone else.

There will always be someone who looks better than we do, has more money, scores better on tests, or has more creative skills. If we're always trying to mimic other people, we won't be looking at ourselves. Imitation may be the sincerest form of flattery, but it keeps us from being ourselves.

We need to stop focusing on what others have that we don't have. We need to look inward at our good qualities as well as our imperfections. We need to see who we are by being ourselves. Life is not made up of people who are good and bad, happy and sad, rich and poor, beautiful and ugly. Life is made up of people being themselves.

I will start to be myself. Help me show others the real me, not an imitation.

The darkness was encumbering only because I relied upon my sight for everything I did, not knowing that another way was to let power be the guide.

—*Carlos Castaneda*

We don't need to be blind in order not to see. Remember how long it took for us to "see" our addictions? Remember how the blindfold of denial kept us from seeing the reality of our lives?

But it took a person or people to help us "see" our way into the program. And now that we are members, we still need others to guide us in our recovery. Sometimes pride gets in the way and tells us we can do it alone, yet those are the times when we stumble and fall. Perhaps today was a day when we refused the guidance of others. We may have felt we were strong enough to "go it alone." But we will feel the effects of such blind gropings if we don't remember that we need others.

Even the blind person has a cane or a companion or an animal for guidance. So we must rely upon the power of the group and our Higher Power to help us "see" our way.

Have I been blind today to the help offered by others? Tonight, can I ask for help to "see"?

It's all right to hold a conversation, but you should let go of it now and then.
—Richard Armour

Do we pay close attention to those who talk to us, or do we spend more time talking to them? How well do we listen to others? Do we hear only what we want to hear, mentally editing out comments and statements from others?

A good exercise to improve listening is to repeat statements said to us, almost as if we were parroting the speaker. It may sound easy, but try it first! Too many of us pay more attention to our thoughts and don't let in words spoken to us. As we think back over the conversations of the day, we may find we cannot recall the things discussed with co-workers, friends, or relatives. We may only recall our parts of the conversations. Can we remember things said at last night's meeting or today's noontime meeting? If we can't, we probably didn't carry much healing or strength away with us. If we begin the listening exercise and use it every day, we may find our growth improving by leaps and bounds, because we've started listening to others.

Help me begin the listening exercise. I will listen as closely as I can to those around me and learn from them.

Some people regard discipline as a chore. For me, it is a kind of order that sets me free to fly.
—Julie Andrews

If we think of the word *discipline,* we might visualize forms of punishment or reprimand from teachers, parents, or bosses. Yet discipline doesn't have to be negative or an effort in blood, sweat, and tears. Discipline can be the structure we need in order to achieve our goals.

Within the program are disciplines to follow to achieve our goal of a renewed outlook on life. The Steps are probably the greatest discipline, for they provide a framework to formulate more positive beliefs about ourselves and our lives. Going to meetings is another discipline that helps keep us on track as we learn and grow. There are other disciplines, too— sharing with others, reading literature, becoming committed to a group, and practicing the program's principles in all our affairs. All these disciplines keep us focused on our ultimate goal: freedom from all past obsessions and negativity. With the discipline of the program, we can learn to fly.

I can discipline myself to remain focused on the program. I know the benefits of such discipline.

It is a matter first of beginning—and then following through

—*Richard L. Evans*

How many times have we started a project or a new path of living only to abandon it after a short time? We may have thought it wasn't what we wanted or there wasn't enough time. Instead of following through, we usually gave up just when it was getting challenging and difficult.

What are our dreams today? Do we wish we could speak a second language, know how to operate a computer, exercise regularly, or attend more meetings? What's stopping us? Each task we'd like to accomplish can only be done by persistence and dedication. We learn a new language one word at a time, learn how to operate a computer one step at a time, exercise regularly one day at a time, and attend more meetings one night at a time.

We don't have to give up an endeavor just because the hard work has begun. Instead of looking down the road where we want to be, we need to look at this moment. If we take a step toward our goals, we'll be closer than if we never took that step.

I can walk toward my goal, remembering each step I take will bring me closer to achievement and personal reward.

Iron rusts from disuse, water loses its purity from stagnation ... even so does inaction sap the vigors of the mind.

—*Leonardo da Vinci*

After a long day of working or doing errands, we may want to sit and not do a thing. But although our bodies may be physically tired, our minds may be just the opposite.

If we're plagued by tired, cranky thoughts after a day's activity, we might discover our minds are too hooked into our feelings. We can separate the mind from the body and learn to chase away stinking thinking. We might treat our tired bodies to a bath while we treat our minds to a good book. While we're soaking our feet or resting in an easy chair, we can put on some music. Or we can put aside the hectic pace of the day and throw our creative energies into preparing a new recipe.

There are countless ways to wake up our minds even if our bodies are tired. Instead of collapsing in front of the television or eating junk food, we can change our focus. We can tune out the signals of the day and turn on our minds.

Did I exercise my mind tonight?

Either you reach a higher point today, or you exercise your strength in order to be able to climb higher tomorrow.

—*Nietzsche*

It has been said truth will set us free. Truth is not simply being honest with ourselves and others. It is also the ideals by which we would like to live. Some people spend their lifetimes never knowing truth, while others search for it in vain. To find truth, we must set out on individual journeys.

In many Eastern countries, people believe truth is found after scaling a high mountain peak and consulting with the guru. In a way, that's what we must do— set off on a tiring journey to consult our Higher Power. Yet our goal is not to reach the top, but to realize truth on the way. As we gain such knowledge, the journey becomes easier and less painful.

No matter how good or bad today was, we have gained ground in our search for truth. We may now have some insights to our lives. Even if we didn't come as far in our journey as we would have liked to today, we still have tomorrow. The search for truth is an ongoing quest filled with great rewards.

Help me find the strength to press onward and upward for truth.

Whatever men attempt, they seem driven to overdo.

—*Bernard Baruch*

It's usually very difficult for us to bring balance into our lives. We may find it hard not to put in overtime at work. We may be obsessed about housework or yardwork to the extent that we work long hours at it. Whatever we do, whatever we have, whatever we want, it's usually not enough for us.

Any activity or commitment needs a certain amount of time, concentration, and energy. But some of us may be too absorbed in physical fitness to notice we are always tense, always on the go. Some of us may be so obsessed with money that we take on additional work, not noticing we are often hard to get along with. Some of us may be so fascinated by a hobby that we ignore people in our lives who need our time and attention, too.

Tonight we need to recognize the obsessive areas of our lives and begin to make changes. It may mean assigning time limits to different activities. Or it may mean altering our schedules, even letting go of an activity. Tonight is the time to begin to bring balance into our lives, gently and gradually.

I know I need more balance in my life. What are some changes I can make to bring the scales more in balance?

So long as we believe we are only human, we are going to experience pain, suffering, tears, disease, and death.

—*Donald Curtis*

Imagine what our lives would be like without negative feelings—fear, worry, anxiety, selfishness, tension, sadness. At first we might feel a great sense of release. But what will we replace those feelings with? What will we feel? Can it be possible to feel happy and joyous and free all the time?

It has been said we experience what we believe in. Do we believe to succeed in this world we have to suffer? We might even believe our sufferings are good: "If I hadn't been hurting so bad, I never would have made that change."

We can try to release the powerful hold our negative ties have on our lives. We can replace those negative ties with warm and loving thoughts, a kind and forgiving nature, and an ability to see good instead of bad. Life doesn't have to be a struggle. We don't have to suffer to be happy.

I can turn over worries, jealousies, fearfulness, and dissatisfactions and look at the other side of living. It is filled with serenity, hope, and light.

Hitch your wagon to a star.
—Ralph Waldo Emerson

How often have we struggled to do something alone, refusing to have another help us? Maybe we single-handedly cooked a meal for a family get-together or moved a piece of furniture or plodded slowly through some confusing work without assistance. Instead of asking for help to make our job go smoother, we chose to take care of it all ourselves. While we probably accomplished what was needed, where did that get us?

Our ancestors settled this land by helping one another. Lands were discovered by bands of exploration parties; barns were raised by communities; crops were harvested by many hands. That same pioneer spirit extends today to the program, where each member pulls another through good times and bad.

Succeeding alone means we have survived; succeeding with others means we have truly lived. We were not put into this life to survive without others, but to live with them. By joining ourselves with the humanity around us, we have joined that spirit which connects us all.

I can be a pioneer and share my humanity with others. How are my brothers and sisters tonight?

FEBRUARY

The Bookshop has a thousand books,
All colors, hues, and tinges,
And every cover is a door
That turns on magic hinges.
—Nancy Byrd Turner

When we start our day, we have a wealth of meditation books to help lead our focus to faith, strength, and hope. Throughout each day, we have pamphlets and books to enrich our minds and expand our understanding of the disease that affects our lives. We learn we are not alone in our struggles and triumphs; there are many before us, many now, and many to come who will ask the same questions, have the same struggles, find the same hope.

Our literature is written by those who, through the help of their Higher Power, can communicate their feelings and thoughts. By keeping a journal to record our thoughts, dreams, feelings, goals, and daily events, we can create our personal book to use for a better understanding of ourselves. This, combined with the literature of the program, will enrich our lives with valuable and inspiring words.

I can begin my record of growth and goals, plans and dreams, and all my feelings. I can be the author of the book of my life.

We should be careful to get out of an experience only the wisdom that is in it—and stay there, lest we be like the cat that sits down on a hot stove-lid. She will never sit down on a hot stove-lid again . . . but also, she will never sit down on a cold one any more.

—*Mark Twain*

"Last night I asked for help, but the person couldn't give it to me. Tonight I'm not going to ask because I'll be refused." Poor us! One person has rejected us, so now we've got the whole world rejecting us. We believe if one person lets us down, everyone else will too.

Such thinking, as negative as it is, can provide safety. If we believe we can't trust anymore, then we won't. But there won't be any growth in this kind of safety. By condemning everyone, we won't see those who want to help.

To find help we may have to ask several people. If we get turned away by a few people, we shouldn't give up hope. There are many flowers in the field of life, but to pick the best, we need to look at them all.

If I get rejected it doesn't mean I'm a bad person or no one can be trusted. It means I need to take another risk or maybe two.

Be strong and of good courage; be not frightened,
neither be dismayed. . . .

—*Joshua 1:9*

It has been said when we are at the end of our rope, we can do one of three things: let go, tie a knot and hang on, or splice the rope and begin again. Whenever we feel there's nowhere to go but down and nobody to turn to, that's when we can start all over again. If we can learn to look beyond the end of something, we'll always see an exciting, fresh beginning.

At the end of every storm is calm. At the end of every argument is silence. At the end of one relationship there is another. Although life is composed of many endings, there are just as many new beginnings. "Life goes on" is even assured by the passage of time—at the end of each minute there's another.

Nights may have many endings, but they will also have just as many beginnings. Just as the sun will set, so the moon will rise and the stars will appear. Just as the day's activities will end, so the evening's activities will begin. And when those activities are over, there will be new experiences the next day.

I can be unafraid of endings because I know they are only the first half of beginnings.

"You silly thing," said Fritz, my eldest son, sharply, *"don't you know that we must not settle what God is to do for us? We must have patience and wait His time."*

—Johann R. Wyss

The story of the shipwrecked Robinson family is a lesson in patience. It was years before their rescue. They didn't know what their fate would be on the unfamiliar island. Yet they survived every day by working together and keeping strong faith in a Power greater than themselves.

We are certainly far from the adversities faced by that family. But at times we may feel our lives would be better if our Higher Power would do what *we* wanted. How many times have we prayed as hard as we could for something we felt we needed?

Today might have been one of those days where we felt our prayers weren't answered. But we need to remember our prayers are heard. Now it is up to us to *Let Go and Let God* work His will in His own time.

Have I tried to be in control of my Higher Power today? How can I Let Go and Let God tonight?

You have to live on this twenty-four hours of daily time. Out of it you have to spin health, pleasure, money, content, respect, and the evolution of your mortal soul. Its right use, its most effective use, is a matter of highest urgency.
—*Arnold Bennett*

We have twenty-four hours to accomplish all we need for mental, physical, and spiritual growth. Just because morning meditations have been read, the work or school day is completed, and the day is waning doesn't mean growth time is over.

The first twelve hours of a day are usually spent housecleaning, raising children, working, running errands, and so on. By the time the activities have ended, we're ready for the second twelve hours: contemplation, relaxation, communication with family and friends, socializing, eating dinner, going to a meeting, sleeping.

Our most effective use of each day means believing we can accomplish something. There is time to be grateful for each day's experiences. There is time to build relationships with ourselves and others. Each day there is time to grow.

How can I use tomorrow to the best benefit?

*God give[s] us a mind that can or can't believe,
but not even God can make us believe. . . . You
have to believe first before you can pray.*
                                   —Harriet Arnow

Sometimes it's difficult to focus on our Higher
Power after a hard day at work, after an argument with
a loved one, after the frustrating experience of a flat
tire, long bank line, or after any of the other nuisances
that are part of each and every day. "Why me?" we
may cry out in frustration. On a day like today, it may
be easier to believe that a Power greater than ourselves
is out to get us.

But God does not choose sides. We have not been
singled out for punishment. God is on our side, if we
only choose to open our hearts and believe that.

As we reflect back on the events of the day, we need
to remember the times we asked God for help and the
times we didn't. And we need to believe first—before
we pray tonight—that God is there to help us every
minute of every day.

---

*Did I ask my Higher Power for help today, or did I decide
to "go it alone"? Which do I choose to do tonight?*

Do not consider anything for your interest which makes you break your word, quit your modesty, or inclines you to any practice which will not bear the light, or look the world in the face.
—Marcus Antonius

Being honest with ourselves and others may be difficult for us. Honesty does not always mean telling the truth. Honesty can also mean knowing our limitations so we don't make promises we can't keep. It can mean letting our actions support our statements. It can mean living for today and not becoming wrapped up in the promises of tomorrow.

How do we feel when people are dishonest? No matter who they are, we probably lose a little trust in them. We doubt their word and don't depend upon them for support. When we are less than honest with others, they may feel the same about us.

Dishonesty may be a quick fix at that moment, but it will never provide a solid foundation for the future. Instead, we can try to be more honest with our abilities and limitations. Honest people attract those who respect them for their honesty.

I can be honest with myself and others about the events of the day and my part in them.

All miseries derive from not being able to sit quietly in a room alone.

—Blaise Pascal

When we are alone, what's the first thing we do? Do we turn on the radio, call a friend, invite someone over, make plans to go out, or turn on the television? How easy is it for us to be in silence for a period of time?

Perhaps we grew up in homes filled with confusion and yelling and everyone talking at once. Silence may be uncomfortable for us. Perhaps we prefer to fill our rooms with noise so we don't feel alone. Whatever method we choose to drown out the sounds of silence, we are also drowning out another sound—the inner self.

How can we possibly think, read, meditate, or write in a journal with noise bombarding us? To learn to sit comfortably alone in silence, we need to try it in small steps. We can start with five minutes, then ten, then fifteen, then a half-hour. By gently easing ourselves into quiet moments, we will allow our inner selves the time and space in which to grow.

I can spend a short time alone in silence, and listen to my inner self.

*Life is like a library owned by an author. In it
are a few books which he wrote himself, but most
of them were written for him.*
—Harry Emerson Fosdick

In our minds there are multitudes of stored memories, knowledge, and skills. Some of these are the results of living and learning, but most are information given to us by others. Our family, friends, co-workers, teachers, and children are the greatest sources for our storehouses of information.

Most of our learning comes from others. Teachers give us much in the way of facts. Our family instructs us in morals. Friends show us different personalities and lifestyles. Our children reflect what we've taught them and give us their views of the world.

All the information we have is valuable to our growth and maturity. Every person we meet, each place we visit, and everything we try contribute to our library of knowledge and experience. At times we may borrow from what is on our shelves, but we must keep our shelves stocked with fresh material. Each night we can write a new volume based on the day's experiences.

I have more valuable contributions to make to my library of knowledge and experience.

When folks have allotted themselves a task und work together in unison, they escape unhappiness.

—Emile Zola

We may have been loners in the past, preferring solitude to the company of others. We may have spent time as children buried in books instead of outside playing with other children. We may have endured high school without lots of dates. We may now feel more comfortable with people in one-on-one situations rather than in large groups.

A meeting is an ideal place to learn how to interact with others. We don't have to act a certain way or hide our feelings, because our group will understand us no matter what. We can give as much as we choose and they will neither harm us, nor ask for more.

By attending meetings regularly, we'll learn they exist because people are working together in unison. Someone "opens up," others make coffee, one will chair and one will speak, and some will clean up at the end. We can learn that the strength of our group lies in the ability of each member to do what is comfortable for him or her. Such coexistence can help us learn we can gather strength from numbers.

I can do something to add to the strength of the group.

If I can stop one heart from breaking, I shall not live in vain.

—*Emily Dickinson*

Many times we may say, "I need a meeting," or "I need to call someone." There are times when other people say the same things because they, too, are in need. The purpose of the program is to help ourselves, but we need to remember others are there to help themselves too. Do we know someone who needs help?

There are so many great rewards in helping another through a time of need. Probably the greatest reward is that we lose our self-centeredness. Helping another through pain or sorrow also lets us help ourselves through our pain and sorrow. We say some helpful things to another that we, too, benefit from hearing.

A third reward is seeing another person's vulnerability. We may find it easier to take risks and expose our humanness by seeing another do the same. Finally, helping another is a way of showing love in a nonphysical way. Many of us may need to learn love isn't only a relationship or sex. Love is gently showing concern and compassion with no thoughts of reciprocation.

I can help another and know there are great rewards in reaching out.

Be aware of yourself and validate your experience. Pay attention to your world, to what's happening, and why. . . . Feel your strength. Value it, and use it.
—Alexandra G. Kaplan

To truly exist in the here and now, we need to feel ourselves in the present. We need to enter each moment without the excess baggage of the past, nor the anticipation of the future.

How do we think or feel in the present? Take away thoughts of other times and we may feel lost and confused. It takes time to learn to live in the present and to trust it. We need to learn that, for as long as we're in the present, we exist. We are.

Imagine the moment as a brand new car. All we need to do is open the door, hop in, and drive away. For that moment, our thoughts will not be focused on cars we used to own or on those we're going to buy in the future. Instead, for that moment, we are in the here and now. That's how each of our moments can be: fresh and clean and exciting.

I can sit in the driver's seat and experience each moment as it occurs. Therein lies my strength.

Have you learned lessons only of those who admired you, and were tender with you, and stood aside for you? Have you not learned great lessons from those who braced themselves against you, and disputed the passage with you?
—Walt Whitman

Wouldn't it be grand if we could have everything our way! We'd have people at our beck and call. We'd never have to take responsibility for ourselves, never have to struggle for anything, never be refused any wish or want.

But how would we mature? Learning involves gains based on the effort we expend. We learned early that we couldn't listen to a music box unless we wound it. We learned we couldn't get good grades unless we studied. And now we've learned we can't change our behaviors without working the program.

If we can't see the results of the energy we put into things, then our motivation, determination, and confidence can't grow. Some things will come easily, some won't. But the things we work on now will mean the most in the end.

I am not afraid to put energy into something I really want. I need to do this for my self-esteem.

I will love you no matter what. I will love you if you are stupid, if you slip and fall on your face, if you do the wrong thing, if you make mistakes, if you behave like a human being—I will love you no matter.

—Leo Buscaglia

Wouldn't it be nice if there were just one person in our lives who loved us no matter what our faults? And wouldn't it be equally nice if we, too, could love just one person in the same way?

Love is not an easy emotion for us to feel. In the past we may have associated feelings of love with negative feelings such as pain, hurt, rejection, or disappointment. But we can put the negative feelings aside and learn how to feel love as a positive emotion.

Love does not necessarily mean sexual attraction or commitment. Love can simply be seeing someone for who he or she is, whether that person is a friend, co-worker, boss, family member, or lover. To show love, we can keep our actions simple—by making a phone call, writing a letter, or sharing a hug. Let's show someone we care.

How can I use Keep It Simple to show someone I care?

People are lonely because they build walls instead of bridges.

—*Joseph Fort Newton*

Remember building snow forts? After a sticky snowfall we'd build a big snow wall. Then we'd mass-produce snowballs, preparing for battle. The team who built the best snow fort usually won, for their wall provided the best protection.

Are we still playing snow fort when we meet new people or spend time with family? Each of us has a wall we started building in our childhood. Each time we were hurt, we would fortify the wall to offer greater protection. We may not even realize it now, but we may have such strong, high walls in front of us that even the most ardent friends can't get over them.

We may feel protected behind our wall, but we may also feel lonely. Walls are built to keep people out. To feel less lonely, we need to make a little crawl space to let people in. We don't have to destroy our walls in one day, but perhaps we can let at least one person in. We will learn, one person at a time, what it feels like to be less protected, and less lonely.

I can make an opening in my wall of protection and let someone get to know me. I will be safe.

*'Tis the human touch in this world that counts,
the touch of your hand and mine.*
—Spencer Michael Free

There once was a girl so afraid of people seeing her sad and lonely that she learned to excel at everything she did. She studied when others were playing so she could get good marks. She practiced sports alone trying to become the best. With all her diligent training, she earned excellent marks and made first-string softball. Her parents thought she was happy and well-adjusted. Yet she was miserable and didn't know how to say it.

How many of us relate to that girl's story? We may have learned at an early age not to share our feelings. Some of us became superachievers; some of us became addicted to alcohol or other drugs, food, or sex; some of us became rescuers for addicts. Yet whatever we became, we always made certain no one touched us or came too close.

We may now accept our feelings, acknowledge them, and share them. We may now be able to let another hold our hands or hug us. We know it's okay to need the human touch.

I can let myself touch and be touched by someone who understands.

We must constantly build dykes of courage to hold back the flood of fear.
—Martin Luther King, Jr.

The definition of courage is the ability to conquer fear or despair. In the past we may have been called courageous because we stayed in circumstances that were difficult or nearly unbearable. We may have felt that walking away from family, children, or friends was cowardly or displayed weakness. We may have felt that by holding back our tears we were stronger people.

Yet all the things we may have viewed as weakness are really signs of courage. All the things we believed to be acts of courage were really not courageous at all. If we walked away from difficult or unbearable circumstances, we would be conquering despair. If we cried, we would have been courageous by letting go of our fear, pain, or sadness.

Courage doesn't mean putting ourselves in stressful or unpleasant situations. Courage doesn't mean controlling our emotions. Courage is the ability to strengthen ourselves against the fear and despair of life, rather than be drowned by it.

What have I done today that took courage? I can be grateful for my courage and strengthen it.

*Be glad you can suffer, be glad you can feel. . . .
How can you tell if you're feeling good unless
you've felt bad, so you have something to
compare it with?*

—Thomas Tryon

How many times have we come home at the end of
a day ranting and raving about how horrible the day
was? Or perhaps our spouse, lover, roommate, or
child has carried home the burden of a bad day. How
can we feel good when the day has felt so bad?

First, we have to change our way of thinking. We
need to apply the old saying "opposites attract" to
those times of stress and unhappiness. We wouldn't
know how to smile if we didn't know how to frown.
We wouldn't know how to cry if we didn't know how
to laugh. We wouldn't even know when we were sick
if we didn't already know what it feels like to be well.

By knowing how things feel—both the good and
the bad—we can be more aware of ourselves. If today
was bad, it's okay to let it go now and know there will
be days that will be good.

*Higher Power, help me to let go of the bad feelings of the
day. Help me to feel grateful for today, no matter how it
has been.*

Reputation is what you have when you come to a new community; character is what you have when you go away.
—William Hersey Davis

All of us in the program have a reputation. We are the children or spouses of alcoholics, or are alcoholics or addicts ourselves. But even though we may introduce ourselves at meetings by our reputations, that in no way reflects upon our character—who we are as people.

As people begin to know us, they learn how we think, what we feel, why we do what we do, what we like or dislike. These things make up character. When we refer to someone as "quite a character," we are referring to a unique personality, a person who stands taller than a reputation.

Do we show others our reputation or our character? Sometimes it's easier to hide behind the walls of a reputation by being snobbish, silent, or sarcastic. Yet it's our character that is far more important. Our character allows us to be who we are and lets us show how we feel. Reputation can make someone look at us, but character can make someone look twice and notice us.

How can I show my character instead of my reputation?

The strength you've insisted on assigning to others is actually within yourself.
—Lisa Alther

If we think right now about people we admire and respect, we'll usually find that their enviable qualities involve a certain degree of strength. So we admire these people, wishing we, too, could be as strong as they are.

Yet each of us has inner strength. This strength defines us as we are and makes us different. We cannot share the same amount of strength in all areas of our life—mental, physical, and spiritual—because we are all different.

Let us think back over the events of today and find our inner strengths. We may work well with people; we may be a good employee or student. As we look around our homes, we may find further clues— handiwork, a tasty meal, flourishing plants, a set of weights, a shelf full of books, a completed crossword puzzle. If we spend less time envying another's strengths and look instead to ourselves, we will have more time and energy to develop our own inner strengths.

What are my inner strengths? How can I make them even stronger?

The twilight, in fact, had several stages, and several times after it had grown dusky, acquired a new transparency, and the trees on the hillsides were lit up again.
— Henry David Thoreau

There are small candles of light we can bring into our lives to take away some of the darkness. These are the candles of the program—soft, warm lights given to us each time we open our faith and trust to the fellowship.

There is the candle we can take home from a meeting, kindled by the caring and sharing of those around us. There is the candle given to us by our sponsors and friends, which burns brighter each time we ask for help. And there is the candle given to us by our Higher Power—an eternal light reflecting strength, hope, and salvation.

It's true that it's darkest before the dawn, but we have countless candles to brighten our night.

How can these candles help me through the night?

Prayer is neither black magic nor is it a form of demand note. Prayer is a relationship.
                                                    —*John Heuss*

A conversation requires two parts: talking and listening. When only we are talking, that is a monologue. When someone lectures, we listen. Prayer can be a form of conversation, yet if we examine the way we pray we may find it's a monologue.

We pray to ask for answers or guidance, to express our gratitude, and to bless those we care for. It's wonderful to open up a channel to our Higher Power by beginning the conversation, but unless we allow time to listen we will never really develop a dialogue.

We can begin to change our way of praying. We can limit our requests so we are not listing a series of wishes or demands. We can ask for patience to listen and then allow a few moments to listen. The answers will come to us and our guidance will be given when we are truly ready to receive them. An equal balance of talking and listening will help strengthen our relationship with our Higher Power.

I will pray and then listen, to allow my Higher Power some time to communicate with me.

*More important than learning how to recall
things is finding ways to forget things that are
cluttering the mind. Before going to sleep at
night, empty your consciousness of unwanted
things, even as you empty your pockets.*
—Eric Butterworth

Many of us may make lists of things we need to do.
We may refer to a calendar for our scribbled notations
of places to go and people to see. We may look over
our course syllabus for chapters to read or papers to
write. Or we may keep it all in our heads, mentally
checking off each item as it's done.

But tonight we can put away the lists, close the calendar book, put away the course syllabus, and empty
our minds of obligations, tasks, and duties. Unless we
want to keep our heads spinning during a sleepless
night, we must learn to turn off the achieving and doing sides of our minds and give room to the relaxing
and spiritual sides. We can take away the items cluttering our minds, one at a time. Tomorrow will arrive
in its own time; tonight is the time for us to relax.

---

*Tonight I can close my eyes and visualize putting aside
each item. I will achieve total relaxation and peace.*

Be patient with the faults of others; they have to be patient with yours.

—Our Daily Bread

How do we feel when someone we know makes a mistake? What happens when the boss makes an error and we have to work overtime to straighten it out? How do we feel when a cashier overcharges us, the post office loses our package, or the mechanic doesn't fix a problem?

Most of us become angry. Since we have been brought up from childhood to believe we are victims, it seems only natural in adult life to feel the same way. We imagine all those people had it in for us; they were all in league somehow to make us suffer.

But everybody makes mistakes. Who among us is perfect? We have made many mistakes in our lives that have probably brought inconveniences to others. If we can learn to treat the faults of others with patience and understanding instead of anger and resentment, we may find others treating us accordingly.

I can overlook the mistakes of others as I would want them to overlook mine.

Love doesn't just sit there, like a stone; it has to be made, like bread, remade all the time, made new.

—Ursula K. Leguin

In the first phases of a relationship, everything is new and exciting. It seems as though nothing could ever go wrong.

Yet as we move out of this "honeymoon" phase of the relationship, problems begin. Suddenly we notice things about the other person that bother us. We seem to have more disagreements and more difficulties that take longer to solve. We may even silently choose corners, put up walls, and back away from each other.

It's easy at this stage to want to end the relationship. But now is when the outcome of the relationship is most critical. If we run away from renewing our love and rebuilding the foundations of trust and faith in each other, we will deprive our love of its nourishment for growth. Love takes constant work and needs plenty of patience. Each day can reveal a new layer of love; each stage in a relationship moves us to a new plateau. But only if we are willing.

———————————

I can look at my relationships and see the potential for growth. Help me renew my feelings of love through faith.

People often say that this or that person has not yet found himself or herself. But the self is not something that one finds. It is something one creates.

—*Thomas Szasz*

In the late sixties, people used drugs and politics to find themselves. The flower children advocated love, not war; they listened to hard rock and political ballads; they looked inward to find out who they were. Yet instead of finding themselves, many seemed to escape from themselves and life.

Many of us today look frantically for ways to discover who we are. We may dress differently or wear makeup. We may consult horoscopes or psychics to gain insight into our being. We may trace our family origins or isolate ourselves in cabin retreats to discover our roots and meaning.

Yet we are not the result of dress or psychic insight or family patterns. We are blank pages upon which we draw who we want to be. Just as an architect draws blueprints for a building, so must we draw blueprints for who we want to be. We are the creators, not the created. We are the artists. Now grab the pencils and let the sketching begin!

I have all the tools I need to create the very best me possible.

We fear to trust our wings. We plume and feather them, but dare not throw our weight upon them. We cling too often to the perch.
—*Charles B. Newcomb*

Even before it has learned to fly, a baby bird is pushed from its nest. It will totter upon the ground, stubby wings outstretched from its body, following the guiding cries of its parents to flap its wings and take flight.

When we were young, our wings hadn't even developed before we began tottering through life. We may have received little direction about how to fly. As we grew, we may have built a nest and retreated within it, still not knowing how to fly.

Although our wings have not been used, we can still learn to fly. There are those who can teach us at meetings. They, too, have had to learn to fly after years of nest-sitting. It isn't easy at first. In fact, it may be quite painful and tiring. But by trying out our wings every day, they will grow stronger and more familiar to us. Our nest will always be there, but we won't have to visit it as often. We'll be too busy flying and testing our wings.

Tonight I can begin to learn the freedom of flight and trust my wings.

*When one knows Thee, then alien there is none,
then no door is shut. Oh, grant me my prayer
that I may never lose the touch of the one in the
play of many.*

—*Rabindranath Tagore*

When we make a person-to-person telephone call, we want to be connected with one particular person. If that person is not in, we make no connection.

Are we taking time to make person-to-person connections? Or are we seeking situations with groups of people so we don't have to be open and honest with just one person? We all need at least one person with whom to share confidences, laughter, tears, hugs, plans, and dreams. If we don't have this special person, we are like one bird in a nest: safe and warm, but isolated and alone.

We can attend a meeting every night and still be isolated and alone. Being around people doesn't necessarily mean we're making connections with them. To truly share ourselves, we need to open the doors to our lives and let at least one person in. Just one person can make the difference between isolation and connection.

I need to connect with a special friend. How can I open the door to this one person?

The preservation of health is duty. Few seem conscious that there is such a thing as physical morality.

—*Herbert Spencer*

How often do we allow ourselves to become hungry, angry, lonely, and tired? When we are feeling those feelings, we are not taking good care of ourselves. And when we're not in good physical health, our emotional health also suffers.

Our past may have been filled with fast food and empty calories or sleepless, caffeine-filled nights. Just as we need to take steps today for our emotional well-being, so must we take steps for our physical being. The first step is good nutrition. We can become conscious of the foods we eat and the vitamins we need. The second step is to exercise our bodies. The third step is to break lonely isolation by making wise choices: attend meetings or spend time with friends. The fourth step is unloading our feelings of anger, frustration, or sadness. The fifth step is to get plenty of sleep.

We can change hungry, angry, lonely, and tired— HALT—with these five steps. We can be renewed!

Tonight I will sleep soundly, for with a healthy mind and body, I can make healthy choices tomorrow.

MARCH

There are no rules of architecture for a castle in the clouds.

—*Gilbert Keith Chesterton*

When we were children and were asked, "What do you want to be when you grow up?" our answers were usually delivered quickly. There was no reason for us to believe our dreams couldn't come true, for we hadn't yet learned fear, doubt, and insecurity.

As we grew older, we began to lose our dreams. We either became overly practical or highly irresponsible. Our fantasies were unable to fly because they were weighted down by doubts. We became negative and cynical. How could we possibly dream of castles in the clouds? Our highly practical side said clouds couldn't hold castles; our irresponsible nature said someone else would have to build them.

We are learning many things are possible now, if we will only believe. We are learning to live without constant fear, insecurity, or hopelessness. We are slowly building health and happiness. Right now, we are also building the foundations to our castles in the clouds. Through time and belief in ourselves, we will be able to build anything we want.

I can be whoever I want to be; dream whatever I want to dream.

For the whole law is fulfilled in one word, "You shall love your neighbor as yourself."
—*Galations 5:14*

Happy and harmonious relationships are essential. If we treat people with uncaring concern and indifference, they will think there are no paths to our hearts. If we meet people with the expectation that they will do more for us than we will do for them, they will turn away from us.

How did we treat people today? Were we short with co-workers or customers; impatient with students, patients, or children; unloving toward friends or relatives? Were we so wrapped up in ourselves that we weren't aware when people around us needed a bit of attention?

We can repair the roads to our hearts so the paths are straight and true. We can rebuild relationships with those around us. If we can help others feel safe, comfortable, and at ease in our presence, we will encourage positive feelings. Then people will feel safe and will turn to us in friendliness and in safety.

What are the messages on the road to my heart? Help me firm the road's foundation with love, peace, and safety.

Here is a mental treatment guaranteed to cure every ill that flesh is heir to: sit for half an hour every night and mentally forgive everyone against whom you have any ill will or antipathy.
—*Charles Fillmore*

What is forgiveness? In a way, it's the ability to let go of negative feelings toward ourselves or others and replace them with good, positive feelings. Are we forgiving to others?

In retrospect, we may discover ill will toward people with whom we had contact today. Perhaps some driver cut us off in traffic and we shouted in anger. Or maybe we snapped at friends, co-workers, or family members. Maybe we nagged at someone whose behavior bothered us. Maybe we carried some resentful feelings toward someone in our past.

Tomorrow, and maybe for several days, we can take time to forgive people for their negative behaviors. After we've done that, we can forgive ourselves for our reactions towards others. Letting go and forgiving is the best way to cleanse ourselves, leaving more room for positive feelings.

Who do I need to forgive? Right now, I can let go of my negative feelings and replace them with good feelings.

Walk with the wise and be wise; mix with the stupid and be misled.

—*Proverbs*

We may not believe we are wise. We may ask, "How could I be wise if I got myself into so much trouble and pain? How can I be wise if I now need the help of others to stay out of trouble and feel less pain?"

But what is wisdom? Very simply, it is good sense. It is the ability to make a choice that will be good for us. No one is born with wisdom. It is learned through trial and error. Just a glance into our past will assure us we have certainly had our share of trials and errors.

We have made a wise decision by joining the program. Because of this decision, our lives have become more manageable and less insane. We have learned of an all-wise Power greater than ourselves. We have become willing to turn our lives and our wills over to this Power.

We have become wise, for those who walk with this Power are wise.

Have I made wise decisions today? How can I use the program to gain greater wisdom?

Remember that you may have and not have. You may receive a property and not enjoy it. You may inherit wealth and not use it. To grasp the great promises of what God can do for you . . . is the way to possess the possessions and realize the wealth.

—H.C.G. Moule

There is so much we have that we take for granted. We seem to focus more upon material things than the wonders of what we already possess. Today we may have wished for more clothes or more money or a bigger house. We may believe more material things will make us better, more powerful, or happier.

Yet we own a wealth of things we never had to buy. We can survive with these things and become a better person. We can take more control of our life and add to our happiness. We were given these things without working overtime or taking out a second mortgage. The wealth we have within us is a gold mine of health, intelligence, and faith. Without these God-given gifts, we are poor in mind, spirit, and body. With these gifts, we truly do have more than money can buy.

Do I realize the value of my mind, health, and faith? I can give thanks for these gifts and learn to appreciate them more.

*It used to be that, if I had a good working day, I
thought I was a wonderful person, but otherwise
I thought I was a terrible person.*
—Byron Janis

How often are we buoyed up by successes and
achievements, only to be let down on an unsuccessful
day? If we do well or have a good day, then we may
feel we're good people. But if our day has gone badly
or we've made a mistake, then our self-image becomes
negative and critical.

No matter what happens, no matter what our
achievements, we're still good people inside. No one
can be wonderful all the time. A good day on the job
doesn't mean we're good, and a bad day doesn't mean
we're bad.

We can look at our self-image and see how we really
feel. Then we can remember we are good, no matter
what we feel. We may not be who we want to be; we
may not act the way we want to act; we may not live
the way we want to live. But we have the power to
change all those things as long as we look inside and
see the way we are. We are good inside.

———

*How do I see myself? Tonight, I can look within and ask for
the courage to see good.*

That's the risk you take if you change: that the people you've been involved with won't like the new you. But other people who do will come along.

—Lisa Alther

When we made the decision to enter the program, it was only a short time before we started making changes. As a result, many of our friends may have become only passing acquaintances; committed relationships may have changed or ended; family members may have become difficult to deal with or may have abandoned us.

Mostly, we have sensed that we "outgrew" those we knew in the past. And we may have been told, "You've changed! I don't like the new you." The excitement and hopefulness we gained with our new way of life were not shared by those who were once close to us. We soon felt alone and rejected instead of supported and accepted by the ones we cared about.

Making changes is risky. But as we become more honest with ourselves and with others, we will soon discover that new people will come into our lives and give us the support we need.

I can become willing to let new people into my life.

Nothing in life is to be feared. It is only to be understood.

—Marie Curie

Most of us have heard older relatives tell of the fears we had in childhood. Many were natural childhood fears; the first day of school, big dogs, even the dark. As we grew older, we understood the fears and grew out of them. Now when we hear reminiscences of those fears, we can laugh.

But what happens when we confront today's fears: meeting new people, attending a social event, giving up an obsession, spending time with our parents? Instead of understanding the cause of our fear, we may let the fear overrun us.

We can put things in perspective by questioning, "What's the worst thing that can happen?" Maybe what we fear isn't always negative. Maybe we fear we'll get that promotion or we won't have an argument with our parents. Whatever our fears may be, we need to see them as lessons to study. Once we understand each new lesson, we'll become masters of our lives. We will run our actions instead of our fears.

I can study at least one of my fears to understand it better.

If one only wished to be happy, this could be easily accomplished; but we wish to be happier than other people, and this is always difficult, for we believe others to be happier than they are.
—*Charles de Secondat Montesquieu*

How many times have we gone out to dinner with friends and ordered what they ordered? Or bought a pair of shoes or some clothing because we liked the item on someone else? Imitation can be the sincerest form of flattery, but it can also be a way of trying to capture the same things we admire in another person.

How often do we compare our emotions? "If only I were as happy as she is," we might say. It may be easier to look at how others feel instead of looking at ourselves. We may not even know how we feel unless we look at someone else for comparison.

Yet appearances are not always the true story. Someone can seem like the happiest person, yet be miserable inside. Happiness has to come from within us. It's okay if our expressions of happiness don't reflect the expressions of others. The only reflections we need to see are our own.

I can look in the mirror and see happiness the way it really is. If I want to be happier, that's up to me.

Little do [we] perceive what solitude is, and how far it extendeth, for a crowd is not company, and faces are but a gallery of pictures, and talk but a tinkling cymbal where there is no love.
—Sir John Lubbock

Today we may be learning what friendship means to us. We may have found that time and the changes we've made have changed the cast of characters in our lives. Friends from the past may no longer be friends; people we never thought we would be close to may now be meaningful to us. Yet we may find it difficult to open up to these people and may hesitate to form friendships beyond a meeting hall or cup of coffee.

Friendship is based totally on trust of another person. Today we are working on trust issues. We are learning we need to take risks to feel comfortable with ourselves and others. Extending the hand of friendship to another or touching the hand extended toward us is the first step in getting to know others and letting them know us.

I can be a friend to another. I can take a risk to share myself and also let someone share with me.

For it is not physical solitude that actually separates one from other men, not physical isolation, but spiritual isolation.
—Anne Morrow Lindbergh

We've discovered that our growth today depends on our mental, physical, and spiritual health. If we picture these as the three legs of a stool, we can see that shortchanging the importance of one or taking one of them away will upset the balance.

We can be at a meeting, for example, yet be unwilling to listen and learn. Or we can bow our heads in prayer at the end of the meeting, yet be unwilling to feel the spiritual strength flowing through the circle of joined hands. By blocking the flow of any aspect of our growth, we are isolating ourselves without even being physically alone.

The remedy to physical isolation is being with others. The remedy to spiritual isolation is opening ourselves to the spirit of life and love that exists everywhere. We can be open to that spirit whether we are alone or with others.

How can I end my spiritual isolation tonight?

Most of us spend 59 minutes in an hour living in the past with regret for lost joys, or shame for things badly done . . . or in a future which we either long for or dread.

—*Storm Jameson*

Do we often travel through life accompanied by the ghosts of our past, present, and future? Instead of focusing on the events in our present journey, we may find ourselves diverted by thoughts of what once was, what we haven't done, and what we may never do.

As long as we travel this way, we will miss a good part of each minute. We will not learn to use our present time to its utmost: to experience, listen, feel, learn, plan, and grow.

The ghosts of the past, present, and future are crutches we lean on when we're too weak to use our own resources. We can be strong if we learn to rely on ourselves, our Higher Power, and our companions in life.

How can I live in each minute without thoughts of the past or future?

The secret to not being hurt like this again, I decided, was never depending on anyone, never needing, never loving. It is the last dream of children, to be forever untouched.
—Audre Lorde

How wonderful it would be if we could never be hurt for the rest of our lives! Imagine never again having to experience the physical and emotional pain of death or loss or change. We might think that all would be well for us, once the potential for any hurt is removed.

Yet hurt is part of the cycle of growth and learning. We had to skin our knees in order to finally ride a bicycle. We had to miss a longed-for event in order to learn how much it meant to us. We had to grieve over the loss of someone dear to us in order to learn how much love we felt.

There are no assurances that we'll never be hurt again. We all feel physical and emotional pain at one time or another. What is assured is that we can ease our pain through the faith and trust we have in ourselves and in our Higher Power.

Have I been living in a never-never land today, shutting myself off from people for fear I'll be hurt?

In returning and rest you shall be saved; in quietness and in trust shall be your strength.
—Isaiah 30:15

By lifting and stretching we stimulate our cardiovascular system, firm up muscles, and add to our strength. But how do we build our spiritual power, increase our strength of belief, build firm foundations of faith, and shape our ability to hope?

Increasing physical power takes time, dedication, and work. So does increasing spiritual power. We need to spend more time in prayer and meditation with our Higher Power, building a strong relationship. We need to work hard at relying upon our spiritual guide to help us in times of need.

We need to awaken and exercise our spiritual muscles by taking Step Eleven every day and night. Prayer once a day does little to improve spiritual power, as sure as one deep knee bend each morning does little to improve leg strength. Just as we would set up an exercise program, we need to schedule our spiritual program. At first it will be hard, but through patience and practice, we will become spiritually stronger every day.

Higher Power, I want to lift the weight in my heart. Help me find ways to develop and exercise my spiritual strength.

Joy enters the room. It settles tentatively on the windowsill, waiting to see whether it will be welcome here.

—Kim Chernin

Is joy a welcome feeling for us, or do we find it hard to express positive feelings? If we grew up in an alcoholic home, we learned early not to trust positive feelings because they usually wouldn't last long. We may have lived with or were familiar with people who had emotional mood swings, and we learned positive feelings didn't have a beginning or end.

Is joy welcome in our lives or do we still fear it? Even if we're still living in an uncomfortable situation, we now have tools to detach ourselves from the behaviors of others. We now have a concept of a greater Power. If we trust the tools and the Power, we can relax and let positive feelings into our lives.

There can be laughter now, perhaps even from us. There are smiles we can respond to and we can initiate some. There are peaceful, loving moments we can experience with others. There can be much joy in our lives, if we can only begin to let it in.

There is joy to feel, if I let myself. What can I feel joyful about in my life tonight?

Few begin with anything like a clear view of what they want to do, and the fortune they seek may come in a very different form from that which they have kept in view.
—The Independent, *August 1898*

Take a look at the most focused and purposeful people we know, and we'll find one common trait. Although most worked toward some goal, they all simply *began* without knowing what would happen. Christopher Columbus set out to prove the world wasn't flat, not to discover the New World. Alexander Graham Bell was fascinated with recording and projecting human voices, not creating a worldwide communications network.

What those people share is the fact that they started. They didn't just sit back and dream. They chose an objective and had faith to begin and follow through, despite repeated failures and years of work. We can dream and fantasize to our heart's content. But we will never realize our aspirations until we take that first step.

What would I like to achieve? Higher Power, I ask for faith to take the first step toward this achievement.

The great rhythms of nature, today so dully disregarded, wounded even, have here their spacious and primeval liberty. ... Journeying birds alight here and fly away again all unseen, schools of fish move beneath the waves, the surf flings its spray against the sun.

—Henry Beston

We think about the many things that are happening around the world. Tonight it is tomorrow somewhere. A new day is dawning, birds are awakening. A rhythm is starting unlike our rhythm now.

Somewhere on the ocean, a supertanker is delivering products to a new location. Beneath it are miles of depth teeming with many varieties of fish. A rhythm is happening that is unobserved.

Birds are flying somewhere in the world right now. There is a nest of eggs with a parent patiently maintaining their warmth. Somewhere there are farmers plowing, children playing, musicians creating, teachers teaching. We are a part of it all. We belong to every creature and every place. We are here—and we are everywhere.

Tonight I can close my eyes and imagine all the life around me and know I am part of it all.

I cannot give you the formula for success, but I can give you the formula for failure—try to please everybody.
—Herbert Bayard Swope

Principles are rules or codes of conduct we set for ourselves; like being honest, striving to be on time, and taking responsibility for bills and expenses. It is up to us to abide by these principles.

When we compromise a principle for someone else's benefit, we jeopardize the strength of that principle and its importance to us. If we want to be honest, then lying to cover up another's actions compromises that principle. If we want to be on time and someone makes demands that cause us to arrive late, we have compromised ourselves and let someone else's desire dominate.

We need to set certain standards for ourselves and abide by them, even if another person will not be pleased. To let principles triumph over the demands and desires of another is a victory for our inner peace. If we are true to ourselves, we will learn we can count on ourselves no matter what.

Is anyone making demands upon my principles? Help me be true to myself and not make compromises I will regret.

*Like the body that is made up of different limbs
and organs, all mortal creatures exist depending
upon one another.*

—Hindu proverb

We may have believed only we could solve our problems and satisfy our needs. Or we may have been super-responsible about caring for others, yet negligent in caring for ourselves. "I'll take care of it," may have been our most-used phrase.

There are some things only we can do for our emotional, physical, and spiritual health: eat right, exercise, get plenty of rest, pray and meditate on a daily basis. Yet there are needs we cannot take care of alone: solving all our problems, comforting ourselves, developing intimacy with others, feeling loved and cared for. Those things need to come from others.

Imagine how dependent we would be on others if we lost our eyesight or hearing or mobility. We don't need a physical handicap to ask for help. We have invisible handicaps that are linked to our emotional and spiritual needs. To mend them, we must ask others for help and guidance. We cannot do it alone.

Tonight instead of saying, "I'll take care of it," I can ask, "Will you help me?"

*You telling me God love you, and you ain't never
done nothing for Him? I mean, not go to church,
sing in a choir, feed the preacher and all that?
. . . if God love me, I don't have to do all that.
There's lots of other things I can do that I speck
God likes. . . . I can lay back and just admire
stuff. Be happy.*

—Alice Walker
The Color Purple

When we were younger, we learned bad people go
to hell when they die. So we may have helped old la-
dies across the street, or didn't kick our brother, or
didn't talk back, or went to church so we could get
"good marks" from the great Power in the heavens.

Today we might still believe our Higher Power
needs material evidence of our faith. We might still go
to church because we think that's what we should do.
We may get down on our knees twice a day because
we feel we should.

All the program asks of us is that we come to believe in a Power greater than ourselves. It doesn't tell
us how to pray or when to pray or the things we need
to do to win our Higher Power's approval. All we need
to do is make our Higher Power a part of our world.

*I can remember that everything is a result of a Power
greater than myself. Can I include this Power in my life?*

Do not lose your inward peace for anything whatsoever, even if your whole world seems upset.

—*Saint Francis de Sales*

Today may have been filled with tense people, hectic schedules, or confusion and anger from those around us. We live and interact with a variety of situations that can range from slightly stressful to very stressful. How we handle ourselves in those situations can determine our inner peace. We can be like an amoeba and suck up the surrounding mood and conform to it, or we can remain detached from the situation and be in touch with ourselves.

Just because the environment around us is like a battlefield or is so uncomfortable we want to squirm, that doesn't mean we have to prepare for battle or move about restlessly. Whatever is happening outside of us is somebody else's issue. Our most important issue is us and our own inner peace. The only way our inner peace can change is if we allow it. We are in control of our inner selves—not the world around us.

I can remain calm and serene in the face of any crises because of my strong faith. I believe all is well with me.

Success is to be measured not so much by the position that one has reached in life as by the obstacles which [were] overcome while trying to succeed.

—Booker T. Washington

When hurdlers race, they look ahead to see each hurdle that must be leaped. High-jumpers see the height of the bar they have to clear. Businesspeople look at charts to see their positions and the number of positions they must pass in order to reach their goals. Students are well aware of the number of credits and course requirements needed for a degree.

Not all of the obstacles in life are as easy to see. Those of us who grew up in alcoholic homes had to overcome tremendous obstacles just to survive. Some of us may have such a low self-image that by just feeling satisfied with an accomplishment, we have overcome tremendous blocks to our growth.

As we measure each day's successes, we need to keep in mind the obstacles we have to face. When we have leaped over a hurdle in life, we have earned a great success. Overcoming one obstacle means there is one less hurdle to stand in our way.

Tonight I can review my day and look for my small successes. I know I have overcome some obstacles today and have done well.

There are parts of a ship which, taken by themselves, would sink. . . . But when the parts of a ship are built together, they float. So with the events in my life. Some have been tragic. Some have been happy. But when they are built together, they form a craft that floats and is going someplace. And I am comforted.
—*Ralph W. Sockman*

If we only remembered the unhappy times we've had, we'd sink into depression. Likewise, if we saw only happiness, we'd have a limited vision of our lives. When we take the good along with the bad, we see reality. When we strive for a balance of opposites, we move closer to maturity. When we accept that for every bad day there will be a good one, we accept life as it is.

There is a saying, *a ship in harbor is safe,* but ships weren't built to stay in harbors. We captain our own ships. When we sail, we are taking risks. There will be calm sailing, but there will also be ferocious storms. We can weather anything with a supportive crew and a determined belief to guide us.

I am not afraid to be captain of my ship. Tonight I can bless all the things in my life that help keep me afloat.

We cannot swing up a rope that is attached only to our own belt.

—William Ernest Hocking

Imagine a drowning person waving for help. A passerby picks up a bundle of rope, tosses it all to the victim, then walks away. That drowning person has no way of reaching safety without another's help. To many of us, that may be a scene from our childhood, where we reached out and asked for help many times, to no avail. Who do we depend on today?

We may not want to place any dependency on anyone but ourselves. But do we truly believe we can provide all the guidance, strength, and hope we need? Even if it is difficult to trust others, we can trust in a Higher Power. That Higher Power doesn't have to be a god; it can be a belief that all is well, that we are doing just what we need to, that we are safe.

By making a connection with someone or something, we can learn to depend on something other than ourselves. When we call for help, we can be rescued only if we believe we can trust another to answer our call.

I can believe I cannot save myself without help. I need to depend upon something or somebody else.

Do not look to small advantages. Desire to have things done quickly prevents their being done thoroughly. Looking at small advantages prevents great things being accomplished.
—*Confucius*

The best work we can do is that which takes time. The ceiling of the Sistine Chapel is the result of years of work. Barns built centuries ago still stand firm. The finest and most brilliant gems are the results of hours of study, cutting, and polishing.

Doing anything well means not merely getting the job done. We are probably very capable of quantity work when we want to be. But it's the quality work—the kind we can step back from and admire today and for years to come—that really counts.

Whether we are working on ourselves, improving our relations with others, or restoring a fine piece of furniture, our best effort is the one that takes time and lasts.

———————

I can work on one thing patiently and thoroughly, knowing the results will be better with time.

One of the most tragic things I know about human nature is that all of us tend to put off living. We are all dreaming of some magical rose garden over the horizon—instead of enjoying the roses that are blooming outside our windows today.

—Dale Carnegie

How we love to think about all the things we want to do! Our lists are probably quite long to include all the things we want, when we have the time or the money.

What are we waiting for? What are our excuses? Many times we make excuses to avoid planning, saving money, or changing schedules. Many times we use our excuses like bricks, building a higher and higher wall until it's impossible to scale. To live is to experience new, exciting, interesting, and diverse things.

To live is to break schedules and change patterns and do things out of the ordinary. To live is to participate in all the fun, all the travel, all the people, all the activities. Are we going to live—starting tomorrow?

I will think about one thing I really want to do and write down what I need to do to accomplish it. To help achieve it, I'll then share this plan with another.

When, against one's will, one is high-pressured into making a hurried decision the best answer is always no because no is more easily changed to yes than yes is changed to no.
—Charles E. Nielson

There are many people we have never refused a favor or help. We may have even sacrificed our time, our schedules, or a friendship to accommodate as many people as possible. Then we entered the program and learned we didn't have to do what everyone wanted. We could say no and that would be okay.

But there may be one or two people we find hard to refuse: a parent or a spouse or an ex-lover or someone we feel we owe. No matter what they ask us, no matter what our schedules, needs, or prior commitments, we may find it almost impossible to say no.

What are we afraid of if we say no? Do we think we'll lose their love or approval, or they'll say bad things about us? We aren't working the program if we can say no to some people and not to others. To be our own persons, we need courage to refuse when we feel it is in our best interest.

I can practice saying no to someone who is difficult for me to refuse.

My world is composed of takers and givers. The takers may eat better but the givers sleep better.
— Byron Frederick

At the end of every Perry Mason show the murderers were caught. Whether their motives were greed, revenge, or justice, their guilt would surface and right would prevail.

Before the program, we may have refused to see our guilt. We may have taken from others because we believed they owed us. But after we entered the program we learned nobody owes us anything. We now tell the store clerks when we're undercharged for a purchase. Our guilt over the dishonesty of taking what wasn't ours would be too much for us.

The giver inside us isn't bothered by guilt and shame. Because we aren't taking from others today, we're only receiving what we deserve. Today, we haven't stolen, lied, or cheated. Tonight we can sleep better because we're givers instead of takers.

How did I give to others or myself today? Tonight I can have a clear conscience knowing I was a giver and not a taker.

I must slowly learn to lose control, to let go the petals when it is time . . . learn step by softly-treading step, that what I am, what we are, is this Power to move and be moved, to change and be changed.

—Linda Roach

Letting go doesn't mean releasing our grip on life and falling into the abyss below. Letting go is a gentle process of easing the grip on some facet of our lives: an obsession, a character defect, or negative feelings toward someone.

We can think of ourselves as pilots flying a plane full of passengers. As we take off and begin our flying pattern, we need to gradually ease the plane into the right coordinates. We can't make a sudden turn, or our passengers will be tossed about. Instead, we need to gently shift directions, bearing in mind the wind as we work our way into the correct path.

We must guide ourselves gradually. We cannot resolve that tomorrow morning we're going to totally eliminate a character defect. But what we can do is become willing to let go. We need to prepare ourselves to change gently, step by step.

I need to remember letting go is a gradual process. With the help of my Higher Power, I can begin to let go.

Here the people seem to possess the secret of tranquility. . . . Perhaps it is only by going up the old back roads leading to the lost little hamlets of the mountains or the seagirt islands and peninsulas of the world that you can still find it. Perhaps even in such places it has not long to last.

—Louise Dickinson Rich

As a child we may have had a secret place we went to be alone or when we were hurt or confused. Wherever it was, we knew we could be safe there.

As an adult we may have lost our secret places. Instead of hiding maybe we learned to run or build up defenses. We learned to cope without secret spaces, but look how we suffered for it! Now we yearn for serenity as we stop running or defending.

We can make a secret space again. Our secret space can be in a favorite chair or even in our minds when we listen to a favorite song. Wherever or whatever we use for times of need, our secret spaces should provide safety and security. It's okay to let the child in us run to secret spaces in times of need. In doing so, we're taking care of ourselves.

Do I have a secret space where I am safe and secure?

Why hoard your troubles? They have no market value, so just throw them away.
—Ann Schade

Some people can't stop talking about their troubles. We innocently ask them how they are, then have to listen to a monologue about this problem and that problem. After a time, we learn to ignore these people and don't dare ask them how they are. We know exactly how they are because they've told us so many times.

We may wonder what those people would say if all their troubles disappeared. They might be speechless, not knowing what to say. Are we, too, afraid to say we're fine? Do we feel uncomfortable not having something to gripe about or focus our energy on?

Troubles are like strings of bangles and beads. They're worthless, don't add much to our appearance, and make a lot of noise. We aren't losing anything by taking off the bangles and beads. In fact, we'll probably look and feel better. We can get rid of the troubles we carry with us as if they were so many bangles and beads. We won't lose a thing by losing them.

I can look at all the troubles I drag around with me and get rid of at least one of them. I'll feel much better without it.

APRIL

*There's sometimes a good hearty tree growin'
right out of the bare rock, out o' some crack that
just holds the roots; right on the pitch o' them
bare stony hills where you can't seem to see a
wheel-barrowful o' good earth in a place, but
that tree'll keep a green top in the driest summer.*
—Sarah Orne Jewett

When our meetings end, we join hands or place our
arms around each other in a circle of prayer. This circle gives us nourishment for our growth, even in ad-
verse conditions.

Without this circle of strength and nourishment, we
would be like we were before the program: a tree
growing shallow roots, searching far for nourishment.
The program grounds us and helps us grow deep and
secure roots.

Whether we choose to grow in a forest or out on
our own, we're never alone. We can survive because of
the spirit that flows through the hearts of program
members into our hearts. Within the protection of the
circle and outside, our needs for growth are answered
and provided for by the program.

*Tonight I can push my roots down deeply and hold
securely onto my space. I've found the place that provides
for my needs.*

A well-timed silence is more eloquent than words.

—Our Daily Bread

How do we handle ourselves when someone is yelling at us for things we consider inconsequential? Do we turn away from words delivered in anger or sarcasm? Do we forgive for hurtful statements? Do we go to another room or leave the scene?

Many of us find it easy to feed into arguments generated by another. Our buttons can easily be pushed by others, and they know it. They expect us to react, screaming at them in anger or crying or defending ourselves. When we're not in the heat of the situation, it's easy to say we'll make changes. But once the scene has started again, our best-laid plans are forgotten.

We can strengthen this change in behavior by learning the power of silence. Responding to a hurtful comment with silence, turning away from another's ire without a word, or walking quietly away from one who is on a tirade can be quite effective. Instead of adding more fuel to an already raging fire, we can cool ourselves off by walking away from the heat without comment. Silence can truly speak louder than words.

I can practice silence in the face of anger or outrage. I can turn away from an unhealthy situation.

Sometimes we need to look hard at a person and remember that he is doing the best he can. He's just trying to find his way. That's all.
—*Ernest Thompson*

Sometimes we need to look hard at ourselves at the end of a day and give ourselves credit for doing our best. We need to look at our actions and reactions as objectively as possible. Now is the time to review and focus on the positive outcomes, not the negative.

The mere fact that we got out of bed, got dressed, and faced the day are sometimes acts of courage and strength. We didn't run from the day; we faced it, even with feelings of anxiety or sadness or fear. What matters is this—that we tried to do the best we could.

Let's look back over the events of the day and remember we did the very best we could to find our own way today.

How did I do the best I could today? What good things have I learned about me?

Sometimes the readiness to be sorry can appear in a flash of insight; other times it may cost a sleepless night or a long sulk. Either way, you've got to go through the process.
—*Laurence Shames*

Making amends—admitting a wrong or apologizing to someone—is never easy. If we are not ready, it really doesn't accomplish much. In order for us to become willing to make an amend, we need to do some work.

We need to feel our way through anger, bitterness, or guilt. We need to recognize and try to put aside our ego issues. We need to become ready to shift from a defensive, battle-ready position to one that is open and honest and sincere.

Sometimes a good night's sleep will help us through even the most difficult of amends. The time spent in quiet rest may help energize us and give us courage and strength to effectively communicate our amends without traces of leftover negative feelings.

Tonight I can let rest and quiet contemplation prepare me to make an amend.

*For peace of mind, resign as general manager of
the universe.*
                                    —*Larry Eisenberg*

How much did we try to control today? Perhaps on
our way to work we shouted in frustration at how
other people drove. Later we may have attempted to
control our boss, co-workers, bank teller, children, or
spouse, telling them to do what we wanted. Perhaps
now we're ready to collapse in exhaustion from a day
of trying to be director of everyone else's play.

Instead of managing everyone else, we should be
managing only ourselves. First we have to catch ourselves when we feel the urge to control others. We
have to discover what is best for us, instead of someone else, and do it. We have to stop focusing on people's problems, even if they want us to. We have to
look in the mirror and see ourselves for who we are.

Tonight we need to realize our director is our
Higher Power, who gives us the play we're in and the
ability to act. Although many other people may share
the stage with us, it's not up to us to direct them. They
have their own direction.

*I will ask my Higher Power for direction, and I will not
control others.*

Often the test of courage is not to die but to live
—*Vittorio Alfieri*

"Against all odds" is an apt phrase for survival despite the worst conditions. For those of us who have lived in an alcoholic home or with abuse or emotional starkness or poverty or handicap, it has been courageous for us to survive despite the difficulties. Yet many times we may feel it would be easier to give up.

But isn't courage survival—despite the odds? When we listen to the stories of our program's members, we need to think of each person as courageous. To live is to grow. To grow well is to strengthen our faith. To have faith is to see beyond ourselves to the completeness of life and our part in it. To be a part of life is to accept what we have and strive to bring what we want into it. To do so is to survive by using the beautiful tools that give us life: hope, faith, and trust.

I am grateful for all I have survived and all I will survive because of my trust and faith in a Higher Power.

I have to laugh at the times I've knocked myself out over a tough spot only to find out afterwards there was an easier way through.
—Robert Franklin Leslie

We receive messages throughout the day that tell us ways of doing things. The door to the store says "pull." The red light tells us not to drive through the intersection. The cereal box says "lift tab and open." Our car gas gauge tells us "empty." With these messages, we are given the guidance on which to base our decisions.

We can choose not to pull the door. Then we'll spend a lot of time and energy pushing until we finally read the sign. All that effort expended, just because we couldn't stop to get some guidance!

The Twelve Steps offer guidance for an easier way through life. We don't have to knock ourselves out over these Steps; all we have to do is follow the direction they give us.

How can I use the Steps to make my life easier?

Each one of us has walked through storm and fled the wolves along the road; but here the hearth is wide and warm, and for this shelter and this light accept, O Lord, our thanks tonight.
—Sara Teasdale

We made it through another day! Sometimes we may feel relief at this statement, other times disappointment, still other times peace.

Tonight we can be grateful for this day. This doesn't mean just giving thanks or recognition for getting something we wanted. Being grateful means recognizing all the events and the people who came our way. It means seeing through disappointments or pain in order to gain understanding of its meaning in our lives. It means trusting everything that happened was given by our Higher Power. We can trust there was a reason for it all.

Giving thanks begins now. We can replay today's events like a tape—watching, listening, and feeling. And at the end of the tape, we can thank our Higher Power for our day, for the people in it, and for the knowledge and experience we gained.

Thank you, Higher Power, for this day. I trust everything in my life today was a gift from You.

We struggle after ideas. We read this book and that, and go from place to place ... instead of pausing to make our own the few great but profoundly simple laws and truths of the spirit.
—Dr. Horatio Dresser

Right now, all we have to remember is that the program teaches us many slogans: *Easy Does It, Keep It Simple, Let Go and Let God, Live and Let Live.* These slogans are more than simple statements. They are truths for our spiritual well-being.

Today may have been a day of intense activity. We may have worked at a frantic pace, but felt we accomplished little. We may then have rushed home to eat a quick meal only to rush somewhere else.

Now is the time to slow down, to stop our frantic pace, if only for a few minutes. We can breathe deeply, let go of all the worries and tensions of the day, then think of a slogan. We can picture how simple it is, yet how truthful its meaning. Now is the time to rest and feel some serenity.

What is my favorite slogan? How can this slogan help me relax tonight?

"And this, too, shall pass away." How much it expresses! How chastening in the hour of pride! How consoling in the depths of affliction! "And this, too, shall pass away."
—Abraham Lincoln

Sometimes, when we're in a dark hour, we may believe time has suddenly stopped. Forever after, we shall always have this pain or sadness or despair. From here on, we think, this is how it's going to be—minute after minute of pain.

But we need to remember time passes quickly when we're enjoying ourselves. When we're in the midst of a negative feeling, every hour seems like two. But this present hour will not endure. Nor the next. Sorrows pass, just as happiness does. Pain passes, just as pleasure does. Nothing really stays the same, nothing ever stands still.

All we need to do, right now, is endure this moment. It, too, shall pass. We need to have strength, patience, faith, and a strong belief that this moment—and the feelings in this moment—will not endure. Time passes, and so will the pain.

Tonight I may need help remembering that this, too, shall pass. How can I let my Higher Power help me?

We need the courage to start and continue what we should do, and courage to stop what we shouldn't do.

—*Richard L. Evans*

What is courage? Many of us think it involves surviving against all odds. Some of us believe courage is personified by an individual like Helen Keller, who coped with many physical defects to vastly change her life and the lives of those around her. Others of us believe courage is personified by people like astronaut John Glenn, who took risks trying something new knowing he could fail.

Are we courageous? Compared to those people we would probably say no. Yet we *are* because we have taken risks to change our lives. Being willing to change is an act of courage. Believing in change and forging ahead on the new, uncharted path is an act of courage.

We are the only ones who can change ourselves. Just as Helen Keller and John Glenn made decisions to alter their lives, so do we make decisions to risk changes. Whether we started on our new way of life years ago, days ago, or even hours ago, we are filled with courage because of the decisions we made.

I can say the Serenity Prayer and remember my courage.

I have wept in the night
For the shortness of sight
That to somebody's need made me blind;
But I have never yet
Felt a tinge of regret
For being a little too kind.

—*Anonymous*

We have only to turn on the evening news to be deluged by all the unkindnesses in the world. Natural disasters destroy and kill. People murder. Governments oppress and torture. People discriminate against others. But if we turn off the evening news and take a look at our own lives—at our relationships—we can see that unkindness is just as prevalent.

Kindness is like a beautiful flowering plant. Pay attention to it, water it, nourish it, tend to its needs, and it will flourish. One flower will open, then another, with a reward of brilliant colors. Show it no kindness, and it will close up its beauty and die.

There are flowers all around me. I need to cultivate my garden with kindness.

Honesty is the first chapter in the book of wisdom.

—*Thomas Jefferson*

We see our true selves when we don't resculpt our bodies, change the style of our hair, or try to imagine someone else instead of us. If we see ourselves as we honestly are, then we will see the imperfections that make us who we are: perhaps too much weight or not enough, a not-so-clear complexion, or being too short or tall. We will never look the way we really want because our desires are usually impossible to attain. We can certainly make some changes, but we need to learn to see an honest picture of ourselves.

The first step to get to know who we are is to know what we look like. We can start by taking off our clothes and standing naked in front of a mirror. That's us, no matter how much we may want to look away or cry or laugh out loud. We may wish that wasn't what we looked like, but that's because we've learned to look at others rather than ourselves. We can take the first step toward wisdom and maturity by seeing our honest reflection, and accepting it.

I will gather up courage to really look at my reflection. I will accept the good as well as the bad.

When they are alone they want to be with others, and when they are with others they want to be alone. After all, human beings are like that.
—Gertrude Stein

We may get discouraged with ourselves because our moods change from one minute to the next. We may make plans for some event we really want to attend, then come right down to the time we're supposed to leave and not want to go. We may feel content with our job one day, then want to quit and go back to school the next. "What's going on?" we ask ourselves in frustration.

Because we're happy and content one minute doesn't mean we're going to feel the same way later. When we're starting on our recovery, our mood swings will be very dramatic. We aren't accustomed to expressing our feelings, so it's only natural that they all want to be heard at once.

It's okay to change our feelings or opinions about something. As time goes on, our mood swings will lessen. But tonight, we need to remember we are growing and experiencing in a way we never have before. Patience with ourselves and our conflicting feelings will help us accept where we are.

I need to remember it's okay for me to feel.

Let us move on, and step out boldly, though it be into the night, and we can scarcely see the way. A Higher Intelligence than the mortal sees the road before us. We do not have to strive for good, but only to go forward and possess it. Good awaits us at every step.

—Charles B. Newcomb

Remember how energized we feel after a good night's sleep, and how a sunny morning helps us forget the bad thoughts of yesterday? We can feel that same energy and sense of hope right now, even though the night is here. The Higher Power we prayed to this morning for strength, hope, and guidance for the day is with us right now, ready to help us relax tonight.

Take a moment to look upon nightfall as a new beginning. Think of new things to do tomorrow. Try a new meeting or volunteer for a group activity. Resolve to start a Fourth Step inventory or ask someone we respect to be our sponsor. New beginnings can happen, if we keep our eyes and ears and hearts open to the messages of our Higher Power.

What good things would I like to have happen to me? How can I use my Higher Power to help me?

I am more involved in unlearning than learning. I'm having to unlearn all the garbage that people have laid on me.

—Leo Buscaglia

What are some of the messages we got while growing up? That we were awful people, or stupid, or unemployable, or lazy, or unlikeable? These messages may have turned into beliefs as we grew older, and we've carried these horrible, negative burdens into adulthood.

Today we may have seen ourselves acting like children again. We may have done or said things to get approval and acceptance. We may have been less than honest with others so they wouldn't see the real us— and perhaps not like what they saw.

We can start to change some of the things we've learned. We don't have to do anything unless it is what we need to do for our healthy growth. We don't have to be someone we aren't. We can be totally honest with ourselves and others even at the risk of possible rejection. We can speak our minds and feel our feelings.

I am in charge of my lesson plan. Who are the ones I choose to teach me?

Finish every day and be done with it. You have done what you could. Some blunders and absurdities no doubt crept in; forget them as soon as you can.

—*Ralph Waldo Emerson*

Are we living in the present, or are we still reliving the past day? If we're still looking backward, there are no surprises, no new wonders. It's like viewing a television rerun—we already know the plot, the characters, and the dialogue.

Today is done. Whatever mistakes, confusions, disappointments, or problems that occurred are also done. Nothing we do right now can alter the happenings of the day. We can best use our time now by paying attention to the present.

Tonight we can look around us at the here and now. We can turn off the reruns in our minds and get set for the new shows to come. We can start fresh and new— right now.

Can I let go of the events of the day?

Worry often gives a small thing a big shadow.
—*Swedish proverb*

Worry does absolutely nothing for our emotional, physical, or spiritual health. Worry makes us anxiety-ridden people. Suddenly a small situation or a minor disagreement takes on the proportion of a giant, looming high above us and casting a long, dark shadow over our lives.

"How important is it?" is a good question to ask at times when we are worried. The second question to ask is, "What can I do about this worry right now?" If we stay in the present, we'll soon discover that much of our worry involves something in the past or something yet to happen. For as long as we focus on the object of our worry, we are not living in the here and now.

We have the power within us to make our worries gigantic. We also have the power to make our worries manageable. As we look back over today's events, we don't need to waste our present time worrying over things done or things left undone. Nor do we need to worry over things yet to come. We can choose instead to live for right now and leave our worries where they belong.

I will walk with my own shadow and not one cast by worry.

Cast thy bread upon the waters: for thou shalt find it after many days.
—*Ecclesiastes 11:1*

There are many conveniences in our lives today. Central heating, instamatic cameras, twenty-four-hour bank tellers, microwave ovens, and shop-by-mail catalogs are just a few of the creations that allow us more time to relax or do what we need to do.

But there are inconveniences, too, that require attention at awkward times. Inconveniences like bank machines that don't work, or hair dryers that break, or airline flights that are delayed. Do we also see people as inconveniences? Perhaps our children need us at inopportune moments or family get-togethers fall during stressful times. If we view such times as impositions, then no time will ever be convenient.

Yet the door we slam may well be the door that is slammed in our face when we are in need. Are we so important that we can't devote a few minutes, a couple of hours, or an evening to someone who needs our attention, comfort, guidance, or companionship? The more we give, the more we shall receive.

Have I viewed people in my life as intruders? Can I learn to give a little to others?

I know that I am here in a world where nothing is permanent but change. . . . I can change the form of things and influence a few people and that I am influenced by these and other people.
—*Elbert Hubbard*

We are related to every person we see in a day, from the bus driver to the family member, from the store clerk to the boss, from strangers on the sidewalk to our dear friends. We are constantly changing, in constant motion with the people, places, and things around us. We are connected like links in a chain. Each link supports and gets support from those around it.

This connectedness is especially evident at meetings when we hear others tell our stories or relate to our feelings. Yet this same connectedness can be felt outside of a meeting with both program and nonprogram people. If there are addicted people in our lives, we can feel a connection with them because of their disease. We can understand them better and see ourselves more clearly through their defects. We are part of a strong chain made even stronger because of our differences.

There are those who know how we feel and can relate to us. I can learn to feel a part of everything.

Prayer is one of life's most puzzling mysteries. I have sometimes feared it is presumptuous to take up God's time with my problems.
—Celestine Sibley

For too long, we may have believed there was no God. Or we may have believed there was an omniscient being who was highly judgmental, ready to bless us when we did good things but ready to curse us when we made mistakes. Our sense of spirituality may have been buried deep beneath layers of fear or lack of trust.

The program teaches us there is a Higher Power who's there to listen to our prayers and meditations. But how do we learn to pray? What do we ask for? What do we say? Do we get down on our knees, bow our heads, or lift our faces to the heavens?

We need to remember that our Higher Power hears us, no matter how we choose to pray. Whether we spend several minutes talking aloud about our day or a few moments sitting still and clearing our minds of all thoughts, our Higher Power cares for us. What's important is making the effort to pray.

Higher Power, help me remember there is no mystery to prayer.

The ladder of life is full of splinters, but they always prick the hardest when we're sliding down.

—William L. Brownell

Climbing is usually difficult—shimmying up a tree, climbing stairs, moving up the corporate ladder, or moving ahead in school. All these actions involve effort and hard work and sometimes may not seem worth it for all the energy expended.

Yet if we failed a semester, lost a job, or fell down the stairs, we'd soon feel the effort was harder. The only payoffs we'd gain from such backward movement would be pain, loss, and abandonment. To pick ourselves up and start climbing again would require almost double the effort to regain the lost ground.

We need to keep moving upwards, keep reaching for the top. Keep on working toward higher goals, dreams, and ideals. It won't be easy to constantly struggle to reach higher. But as long as we don't look back or fall back, our lives will be filled with rewards. By moving ever upwards, we cannot fail.

There's no going back to the pain and hurt. I need to keep moving up, up, up.

Man is born broken. He lives by mending. The grace of God is glue!

—*Eugene O'Neill*

Has today been a day when we felt like we've fallen apart, faltered in our sense of direction, or lost confidence in ourselves? Tonight we may feel like we just can't get it together—that it would be better for us to curl up in a tight ball and wait for a new day.

But the dawn of tomorrow will not work miracles upon us. It is up to us to get us back on track. When our shirt loses a button, we don't throw away the shirt. We use a needle and thread and a little bit of patience to sew the button back on. The work we put into the shirt doesn't have to be perfect, it just has to make the shirt wearable again.

Tonight we need to take time to mend ourselves. And we have the tools to do this—our Higher Power, literature, and meditation. These are our needle and thread. Through the grace of God, we've been given all that we need to mend ourselves.

How can I use the tools of the program to rebuild myself?

Being sorry for myself is a luxury I can't afford.
—Stephen King and Peter Straub

We have surrounded ourselves with many luxuries to enhance our lives: microwave ovens, color televisions, clothes, jewelry, and so on. We may have purchased these items even if we couldn't really afford them—just as long as we could have them and use them.

Some of the things that are also important to us are our negative emotions: depression, self-pity, selfishness, ungratefulness, or anger. But what if we had to pay for the luxury of feeling each of these feelings? Would we be able to afford a week of self-pity? An hour of anger? Or several minutes of selfishness?

The value we place upon the material things in our lives can also be placed on the emotions we feel each day and night. Our positive emotions can enrich us, but our negative emotions will leave us in debt.

Am I rich enough to waste time feeling sorry for myself? How can I use my resources wisely?

Ignorance is the night of the mind, but a night without moon or star.

—*Confucius*

Long ago, before the advent of radar systems, navigators and explorers found it impossible to proceed on cloudy nights. Without the moon or stars to guide them, they lost their sense of direction and the light by which to see. They were powerless and had to accept their inability to progress under such conditions.

Tonight may seem like a cloudy night. We may feel lost or directionless, or we may feel as if we've stayed in the same emotional space. We may pray in desperation for movement and change, only to feel as if our prayers go unanswered. Like a car mired in mud, we may be spinning our wheels and going nowhere.

Acceptance, then, is our answer. Just because our prayers haven't brought the results we've wanted doesn't mean no one has listened. Our prayers were heard, and the answer was to stay where we were and wait. Our journey is being prepared for us. Soon the clouds will roll away, the moon and stars will guide us. Our Higher Power's will, not ours, is what we have to accept.

Even though I may feel like I'm going nowhere, tonight I can turn my life and my will over to the care of my Higher Power.

If you have knowledge, let others light their candles at it.

—*Margaret Fuller*

We are seen as powerful examples every time we speak at a meeting, offer encouragement, and give support to those in need. The knowledge we've gathered from the strength and hope of the program is a gift to share with others.

If we've ever seen a candlelight ceremony, we know how powerful one candle can be. Countless tapers can be lit until a room is brilliant with light. Our knowledge of the program is kept alive by a tiny candle within us. And each time we share our knowledge, we have the ability to light the candles of others.

Sometimes we may feel our faith and hope lessen and our candlelight begins to flicker and dim. Yet we can light our faltering candles again from the knowledge of another. We are all candlelighters to each other. This gift assures that we'll never be in the dark. We'll always have the ability to gather light and to give it.

I will let others light their candles from mine, thereby sharing the light of the hope in the program.

Everyone needs optimism. If you don't get it inside you get it outside.
—*Dr. Denis Waitley*

What made us feel optimistic in the past? Perhaps our use of drink, drug, food, or relationship helped us feel optimistic. Perhaps another person's behavior made us feel optimistic. But these feelings probably didn't last long because they were based on persons, places, or things outside of us. As soon as those things changed, so did our feelings.

Today we're learning who we are and what it's like to feel. We're learning to appreciate solitude and our own company. We're learning that feelings come from within. But how can we feel optimism from within us? How can we cultivate feelings of hope?

We can look at how different we are than when we first came into the program. We can also gain optimism by looking at the changes in those around us. Observing abstinence, behavioral changes, and fewer mood shifts are sure signs that the program works. Optimism can grow within us by seeing and hearing growth in ourselves and others.

Can I feel optimism about my growth? Can I see positive changes made by others in the program too?

There is something infinitely healing in the repeated refrains of nature—the assurance that dawn comes after night, and spring after the winter.

—Rachel Carson

Sometimes it seems as though time speeds up during fun-filled hours and slows down during times of idleness, misery, or pain. But time proceeds at a steady, unchanging pace. Because of this, we are assured that with every minute there can be new hope. Bad times will end with the great healer—time.

Time brings summer to a close as well as winter to an end. Time ages the brilliant petals of flowers as well as prepares the new buds. Time brings the end to a life as well as the beginning to another. Because of this continuum, we can trust that time will bring the good to us as well as take away the bad.

Today may have been a trying time. But tomorrow will dawn and along with that dawn comes renewed hope. We can trust in the constancy of one thing— time will always move forward, taking us away from the old and gently guiding us to the new.

Time is always on my side, taking me ever closer to new moments that are fresh and untouched. Tomorrow will give me many such moments, of this I can be assured.

As a girl my temper often got out of bounds. But one day when I became angry at a friend over some trivial matter, my mother told me, "Elizabeth, anyone who angers you conquers you."

—Sister Elizabeth Kenny

The phrase "seeing red" is appropriate to describe anger. It may be comfortable for us to feel anger, or it can be excruciatingly painful. But unless we know how to get rid of our angry feelings and bring our lives into balance, anger will dominate us and color everything we come into contact with.

How do we stop feeling angry? The program gives us many ways. First, we can accept our powerlessness over the person, place, or thing that caused our anger. Second, we can ask, "How important is the cause of this anger? Will it be significant enough to remember weeks, months, or even years from now?" Third, we can ask our Higher Power to help us let go of the anger. That may not be easy, for we may want to hold on to it almost as much as we'd like to let it go. But with practice, we can learn to conquer our anger instead of having it conquer us.

Am I angry tonight? I can use the Steps to help conquer my angry feelings and to stop seeing red everywhere I look.

Keep watch over your ability and prudence, do not let them slip from sight. . . . Then you will go your way without a care, and your feet will not stumble. When you sit, you need have no fear; when you lie down, your sleep will be pleasant.
—*Proverbs*

When we lose our confidence, it's easy for us to doubt if we're good at anything. Today may have been a day where nothing seemed to go right. It's easy to blame ourselves for the people, places, and things that were out of our control.

As we look back over today, we may find we've blamed ourselves for things absolutely out of our control: another's anger, poor communication, or a general mix-up of everything. But just because things didn't work out perfectly doesn't mean we've lost our God-given abilities and talents.

We have capabilities that make us special. Through the program, we're beginning to see we are good at many things. It's not fair to want to throw all those beautiful talents out the window whenever things go wrong—not fair to *ourselves.*

Tonight I can affirm that I have special talents and abilities. Can I list at least five of them?

MAY

The first sight of the lighthouse set boldly on its outer rock, the flash of a gull, the waiting procession of seaward-bound firs on an island, made me feel solid and definite again, instead of a poor, incoherent being. . . . It was a return to happiness.

—Sarah Orne Jewett

Many of us have things that calm us, center us, bring us inner peace. For some it is the ocean, with its smells, sounds, rhythm, vastness. For others it is a spectacular sunset, where luminous colors spark each surrounding cloud into an ethereal hue. Still others may have a song that gives peace and comfort.

These are our positive relaxation "fixes." When we have been away from the ocean for a while, we have an urge to go again. Just seeing the ocean is reassuring and soothing, as is the sunset or song we seek for comfort.

Our ability to recall is a wonderful gift. By closing our eyes we can see relaxation, hear it, touch it. We can create it clearly in our minds. A few minutes of such meditation can do hours of good.

What relaxes me and makes me feel good? Tonight I will think about that pleasant thought and feel the peace and contentment it gives me.

*Weigh thy words in a balance, and make a door
and bar for thy mouth.*
—Old Testament apocrypha

What we say can hurt or heal. We may look back at times and wish we hadn't said something to someone. Perhaps we can see the hurt we caused by harsh or insulting words. We may be able to recall a snide or impatient comment delivered to an unsuspecting stranger or friend. Words can be powerful weapons.

By the same token, we may be able to recall when someone said, "Thanks. I really liked what you said to me. It helped." We may have made someone laugh or smile despite tears, or we may have been able to point out a different viewpoint to someone blinded by rage or impatience. Words can be powerful healers.

Freedom of speech doesn't mean we can say anything we want whenever we want. Communication is an action that requires responsibility. Abuse of speech can lead to angry confrontations, severed relationships, and isolation. The responsible use of our gift of speech can lead to healthy relationships and positive emotions. We can listen to ourselves and learn whether our voice helps or hurts.

My words can hurt or heal. Which will I choose?

Go ahead with your life, your plans, your preparation, as fully as you can. Don't waste time by stopping before the interruptions have started.

—Richard L. Evans

Inside each of us is a little voice called "Too Cautious." Too Cautious loves to be the initiator of doom, the forerunner of disaster, the messenger of disappointment. When we start to plan our vacations, for example, Too Cautious will tell us we don't have enough money, or we probably won't get a reservation, or we've got too many other things to do. If we think about going back to school, Too Cautious will tell us we won't have enough time or we'll probably flunk. If we want to ask a friend to do something with us, Too Cautious will whisper in our ears that we aren't likable and will probably get refused.

But we don't have to listen to Too Cautious. We can listen instead to our Higher Power. We'll soon hear inspiring words of faith that will help us take more risks, like "Why not?" or "Wouldn't that be nice?" or "What a wonderful idea." We can listen to our Higher Power for strength, hope, and guidance in all our affairs.

What's stopping me from making plans or taking a risk?

My father taught me that a bill is like a crying baby and must be attended to at once.
—Anne Morrow Lindbergh

In the past, we may have faced our bills with denial or justification that we needed the things we had purchased. We may have abused credit cards so much that we are still paying for items we purchased months or years ago. And we may have problems today with spending more than we earn.

Many times material wants are based on emotional needs we don't know how to satisfy. In the past we may have thought we could ease our pains and troubles by buying new clothes or a bigger stereo. Our emotional needs are still screaming for attention and it may be difficult to stop using material purchases as pacifiers.

Like the recovering alcoholic who avoids a drink, we must disregard temptations of credit cards, extravagant purchases, and borrowing. Material things provide only a temporary reprieve, they will not take away our emotions. Emotions can only be eased by things money can't buy: time, love, faith, and understanding.

I don't need to buy anything to take away my feelings. I can attend to my feelings with the tools of the program.

You would do well to budget your time as follows: one-half in work, taking care of personal belongings, etc.; one-fourth in social pastimes with others, both young and old; and one-fourth as an interested, pleased observer of life.
        —William B. Terhune

Every life needs a balance of work, play, and rest. When we're not at work, we need to pursue other interests like hobbies, socializing, going to movies. When we're not at work and not pursuing an interest, we need to rest. Resting doesn't mean just sleeping. Resting is also meditating, listening to relaxing music, or watching the birds at our bird feeders.

Our financial budget tells us where our money is spent. Our time budget can do the same thing. By noticing where we spend most of our time, we can make sure all our time isn't spent doing just work, just play, or just rest.

I can look at my time budget and ask: "Where haven't I spent any time lately?" I need to use my time doing something I haven't done to balance my budget.

*It has never been, and never will be, easy work!
But the road that is built in hope is more
pleasant to the traveler than the road built in
despair, even though they both lead to the same
destination.*

—Marian Zimmer Bradley

Think for a moment about a city nearby. Now picture the many roads that lead to that city. One may be a winding road. One may be an expressway. No matter which one is taken, it will still reach the same destination. But what will matter is how pleasant the journey is along the way.

Before we entered the program, we probably traveled on the road marked *despair*. We didn't know there were other roads for our journey. But the program has taught us there are many roads to recovery: *strength, hope, peace, happiness, caring,* and *love*.

As long as we keep recovery as our destination, we may choose to travel any road of the program we like. If we've traveled today on the road called *despair*, we can change our road tonight to one of *hope*. As long as the program is our destination, we need not worry about losing our way.

Which road will I travel tonight? Where will this road lead me?

*Don't waste your time striving for perfection;
instead, strive for excellence—doing your best.*
—Sir Laurence Olivier

We've all heard that even the most beautiful rose has its thorns. But as that rose was growing, the gardener didn't waste time trying to snip off the thorns. Instead, by using the right combination of sunshine, water, and nutrients, the gardener knew the rose would grow healthy and strong.

We are both the rose and the gardener. We are beautiful, yet we have our thorns—our defects of character. We may have seen some of those thorns showing today. But as gardeners we have some very special tools for our growth: the program, the Twelve Steps, the slogans, and the fellowship. By using these tools, we are assured of healthy growth.

We will always have our thorns. But we can still be beautiful as long as we tend to ourselves with patience, love, and the proper tools.

Did I try to strive for excellence today? How can I use the program to help my growth?

Reach high, for stars lie hidden in your soul.
Dream deep, for every dream precedes the goal.
—Pamela Vaull Starr

It has been said that if we tell ourselves what we'd like to dream about before we go to sleep, we can teach ourselves to dream our own dreams. Rather than letting our confusing dreams puzzle us or our nightmares frighten us, we can train our minds to think positive thoughts while we're resting. After a night of positive dreaming, we are more likely to wake up refreshed and ready to continue thinking positively.

Tonight we can prepare our dream by visualizing what it will be. We can close our eyes and see ourselves doing whatever we want to do or be whoever we want to be. Immediately after this visualization, with it fresh in our minds, we can then lie down to sleep with the positive thoughts of the dream in our heads. Such positive thinking is one giant step toward an affirmation of ourselves.

What will I dream tonight? I can imagine the most positive thing and let it become a part of my sleeping thoughts.

How many times have we heard, "Why? I've given him the shirt off my back and now look what he has done to me," or "I've given him the best years of my life and look what I get in return." If we bestow a gift or favor and expect a return for it, it is not a gift but a trade.

—Anonymous

It's not easy to give to another with no thought of return. In the past we may have given to takers who drained us of money, food, and time. We may have felt we were supposed to give and give some more.

Then in the program we learned we could receive and didn't have to give all the time. We may have then become overly conscious of giving. We may have been so adamant about not being taken advantage of that we became afraid to give.

Through our growth in the program, we may find it easier to see the difference between a taker and a true friend. In so doing, we'll find we don't need to measure our giving. It will come back to us from those who are truly worth giving to.

I can give to the people I know won't hurt me or take advantage of me. I can trust them.

Ozone and friendship will be our stimulants—
let the drugs, tobacco, and strong drink go
forever. Natural joy brings no headaches or
heartaches.

—Elbert Hubbard

The longer we stay in the program, working on bettering ourselves, the more addictions we'll find we've outgrown. The alcoholic and the drug addict learn life can be grand without chemicals. The overeater acquires an appetite for fresh air and companionship rather than food.

When we learn to see our lives without a primary addiction, we can then rid ourselves of secondary addictions like smoking, obsessive exercising, caffeine, and sweets. We can free ourselves from all addictions and have a more serene outlook on the healing power we have over our lives.

However, we need to remember we can be obsessive about change. We don't have to become a natural-food freak or a lecturer on the evils of white sugar or nicotine. But we do need to look at the hold those addictions have on us. When we're ready to let go of an addiction, we'll let go of it freely.

I can look at the addictions in my life and make some
changes. I can begin tonight by working on letting go.

A mother's heart is the child's schoolroom.
　　　　　　　　　—*Henry Ward Beecher*

We've learned much from our mother. That doesn't mean all our learning has been good or wise, just as it has not been all bad or crazy. Where we are right now in our lives is a result of the things we have learned thus far.

Mothers aren't perfect. Our mother had a mother who taught her. What our mother did was cope as best as she could with what she was taught. We probably received the best she had to offer, even if it may not have been the best in our eyes.

As we look back to our school days, we need to keep in mind that we haven't retained all the information we were taught. We've kept the most interesting and beneficial textbook learning so we could make our way in the world. The learning we received from our mother can be treated in the same manner. Tonight, we can recall what we like and leave the rest. The most beneficial learning she gave us could be as simple as knowing how to tie our shoes or bake bread, or as all-encompassing as our ability to believe in ourselves.

Tonight, I can thank my mother for the good things I learned from her.

Love is a great thing, a good above all others, which alone maketh every burden light. Love is watchful, and whilst sleeping still keeps watch; though fatigued, it is not weary; though pressed, it is not forced.

—*Thomas à Kempis*

Love is not just something we say or write. Love is the face we put on, the clothes we wear, the way we walk and move—our very heart and soul. If we are not made up of love, we will reflect this to others and will feel it within ourselves.

Love isn't just a feeling. Love is a truth filled with forgiveness and kindness; with generosity and honesty. It is the willingness to serve and protect, to cherish and respect, to honor and be strong. We do not have to have feelings of love for everyone we meet, but we do need to love them.

Have we loved those around us today? Have we shown others that we acknowledge their truth and character, in the same way we would want them to acknowledge us? If we can see love as separate from the feelings of falling in love, we will then begin to understand there is love in all of us. And each of us is special enough to be loved.

Tonight I can see love is everywhere and in everyone.

We live on a moving line between past and future. That line is our lifeline.
　　　　　　　　　　　　　—George A. Buttrick

Live in the present is a good slogan for those of us who grew up in an alcoholic family because many of us find it hard to do. Sometimes it feels like everything we do is a result of the way we were brought up, and those memories can come flooding back no matter what we're doing. Our character defects, fears, actions, and defenses were all constructed before adulthood. These influence us in the present.

Because of our childhood, we are also future-oriented dreamers. We learned to look forward to times when our worries, fears, and pains would be gone. That always seemed to be tomorrow. Everything would be all right—tomorrow.

The past is behind us and the future lies ahead. We are learning the present isn't as painful, as fearful, or as uncomfortable as the past. We may look to the future for hope, but not to place all our faith into a future moment. The present is not so bad, as long as we remember it will never be repeated and our future will never be an unattainable fantasy.

I can place all my faith, trust, and hope in the present.

The pessimist sees the difficulty in every opportunity; the optimist, the opportunity in every difficulty.

—L. P. Jacks

How many times have we opted not to do something and listed countless reasons? Perhaps we've rejected a career change or geographic move or promotion. Or maybe we've passed up get-togethers or renewing friendships. What is it that tells us to say no?

Looking back, we may discover we've refused changes in our lives because we'd lose our security. We may have refused friendly offers because they meant sharing ourselves with others. We may find that all we could see were difficulties coming out of change and not any enjoyment.

Yet there are riches in every opportunity that comes our way. Our Higher Power doesn't put anything in our path that won't help us grow and learn. By seeing opportunities only as difficulties, we are stifling our enjoyment, growth, and pleasure. If we learn to see more opportunities as great learning experiences, we may begin to say yes.

There will be opportunities that come my way. Help me learn to say yes to them.

We owe to our first journeys the discovery that place is nothing. At home I dream that at Naples, at Rome, I can be intoxicated with beauty and lose my sadness. I pack my trunk, embrace my friends, embark on the sea and at last wake up in Naples, and there beside me is the stern Fact, the sad self, unrelenting, identical fact that I fled from.

—Ralph Waldo Emerson

Many times we may not like what we are thinking or feeling or the way we are acting. We may try to run away, hoping a geographical move, or new job, or new set of friends will make being with ourselves more bearable. Yet no matter how we change our environment or lifestyle, those changes will not change us.

We can become more bearable by changing from within. If we don't like the way we think, perhaps we can take one minute tonight and think positive thoughts. If we don't like the way we act, we can begin changing our behaviors. By changing from within, we will deal with the reasons why we want to run from ourselves. We will change the person we are running from.

I can stop running and start looking at myself. How can I make myself more likable to me?

If you don't have such a clear picture of what
you want, you may become more humble.
—Carlos Castaneda

When we were growing up, our parents often wished our career definitions would be specific: fire fighter, teacher, police officer, doctor, lawyer, nurse. Yet as we grew older, we may have questioned such cut-and-dried choices. We may have gone to college and majored in a subject not defined by a career. We may have chosen the business world for financial reason. We may have enlisted in the military or gotten married.

Who are we now? We may just be beginning to question who we are and what we want from life. We may be dissatisfied by our choices of the past and are yearning to redefine our goals.

We are changing every day. Such change has given us room to grow because our definitions of ourselves are not so clear, so rigid. Our work on Step Four teaches us to take continual inventory of ourselves. This personal inventory has enabled us to remain forever humble as we realize we are ever-changing, ever-growing persons.

Tonight I can be grateful for the freedom in which the program allows me to grow.

Imagine how little good music there would be if, for example, a conductor refused to play Beethoven's Fifth Symphony on the ground[s] that his audience may have heard it before.
—A. P. Herbert

Long ago, before printing presses, telephones, and instant replays, our ancestors kept records of people, information, and history by telling the same stories many times. These stories were passed down from generation to generation. People crowded into caves and huddled around roaring fires to hear the old stories. They never grew tired of hearing them, for with each telling could come a new insight and a renewed interest.

When we hear the same things, we can tune in instead of tuning out. We can listen to each word as if it were the first time, feeling all the feelings and leaving our minds open to new insights. Perhaps we can garner a few lines to include in our own storytelling or that relate to us in particular. Conversations and stories can be the same with each telling. But we can keep them fresh by listening differently each time.

As I lie down tonight, I can imagine I've regained my hearing after years of silence. I can begin to listen as if it were the first time and gain so much more.

After 8,000 unsuccessful trials on a nickel-iron storage battery, Thomas Edison said, "Well, at least we know 8,000 things that won't work."
—Robert Millikan

If we don't believe we will be successful, all our efforts are doomed from the start. If we fear success or prefer the norm, we will not want to succeed. If we've been let down many times before, once more will make us want to give up. The bottom line is: How badly do we want to succeed at our goals?

Thomas Edison worked eagerly to discover the battery. He looked at his unsuccessful attempts not as failures but as information. He turned what some may see as failures into successes even though he didn't achieve the results he wanted.

If we want something desperately, we can choose to do all we can to get it. We can change our attitudes about the results by looking at them not as failures but as accomplishments. Then we can try a new way and not give up until we have exhausted all possible ways. If we work hard at it, we will be successful.

Tonight, I can keep a positive outlook and a strong determination.

Happiness is knowing that you do not necessarily require happiness.
—*William Saroyan*

Do we believe happiness comes from material things? Yet stereos break down, clothes become worn, and cars attract scratches and dents. Do we believe we will be happy with a promotion or move? Yet new jobs and new homes soon become old jobs and old homes. We'll yearn again for another change, another challenge.

The struggle to attain happiness becomes easier when we realize we can be happy without having to struggle for it. We can be happy just by knowing we don't have to have the new car or the new home or perfection in our lives. Our happiness can come from just being ourselves, living each day, doing what we need to do for ourselves. To be happy means we don't need to struggle to find happiness.

Tonight I can be happy with myself and where I am right now.

You just have to learn not to care about the dust-mice under the beds.

—Margaret Mead

Perfection is something many of us strive for. We want the perfect marriage or relationship. We want the perfect house and perfect clothes. We want the perfect job and we yearn to be the perfect employee. We want perfection in our personalities and in all our actions.

Perfection means being perfect—no faults or blemishes. Sometimes we see perfection by a gymnast who scores a perfect ten. Yet every time that gymnast performs, she doesn't always score a ten. She is not perfect all the time, or even most of the time.

We can experience momentary perfection. Perhaps we earn an "A" or write a faultless business proposal or complete a knitting project without a dropped stitch. But these accomplishments don't mean we will always be perfect. We need to see ourselves as imperfect and allow the dropped stitches, the "Bs," and the 9.5 scores to exist. They let us see we are perfect in a special way—we are perfectly imperfect human beings!

Nothing has to be perfect, as long as I give it my best effort.

She looked around and found there were no monsters, only shifting shadows from the play of moonlight through the trees outside the window.
—Lisa Alther

How often have we heard a child's bedtime fears are the result of an overactive imagination? Our own imagination can run wild at night, to such an extent that our reality becomes distorted. We begin to imagine things that are not real.

If someone doesn't say hello to us, we may think that person hates us. An unreturned telephone call could signal that another has stopped being our friend. Instead of seeing what really exists, we let our imagination take over. Minor inconveniences become major catastrophes; small sounds become amplified into "things that go bump in the night."

Tonight is as real as today. There is nothing to fear except the thoughts in our own minds. And we can chase those away by remembering to look at things the way they really are, not as we imagine them to be.

Tonight I can use my mind to see clearly. Darkness cannot cloud my thoughts.

Sometimes I feel mad at her. Feel like I could scratch her hair right off her head. But then I think [she] got a right to live too. She got a right to look over the world in whatever company she choose. Just cause I love her don't take away none of her rights.

—Alice Walker,
The Color Purple

When we open ourselves up to caring, sharing, and giving, we also bare our vulnerable spots. We often hear how beautiful it is to be in love, but we also know how painful it can be.

We might not mind being in love if the other person would stop hurting us. Sometimes it seems deliberately done: coming home late for dinner, forgetting an appointment or special event, or falling asleep when we want to be intimate. We may then express our hurt in ways that will hurt the other: yelling, throwing things, hitting, running away, breaking up.

Sometimes we forget important dates or are too tired to express intimacy. If those are our rights, then they must also be the rights of others. To truly express love, we need to have room to grow as two beautiful flowers, instead of one depriving the other of light and nourishment.

I can give space to a loved one.

The soul is dyed the color of its thoughts.
—*Marcus Aurelius*

If we give a group of children paper and crayons and ask them to draw a self-portrait, we will see that their choice of colors will communicate how they feel about themselves. Pastel colors can convey happiness and contentment; bright colors can reveal strong feelings; black or blue can mean sadness or pain.

How would we color a picture of ourselves tonight? If our day has been good and we've kept our thoughts positive and focused in the present, our choice of colors will probably show contentment and serenity. If our thoughts today have been negative or focused on the past or future, we may choose colors that reflect confusion, fear, sadness, or insecurity.

We can steer clear of the blues tonight if we think of ourselves in happy colors. There's a whole rainbow of colors to feel—the choice is up to us.

What color is my soul tonight?

Tension is a habit. Relaxing is a habit. And bad
habits can be broken, good habits formed.
—William James

Nail biting, foot shaking, hair twirling, finger tapping, and hand wringing are all ways of showing nervous tension. We most likely have these habits unconsciously. To stop, we can use the tools of the program as if we are breaking an obsession. We can use the slogans and Steps to give us first the awareness and then the strength to break the nervous habits. We can also learn good habits with which to replace the old.

For example, we may be very nervous before a meeting starts. So we sit there biting our nails, perpetuating the bad habit. We can replace that bad habit with a good one like volunteering to make the coffee. By doing so, we'll keep our hands and minds busy until the meeting begins. By using the program to deal with bad habits and choosing positive replacements for them, we can change our bad behaviors into good ones.

What are some of my bad habits? Tonight I can think of good habits to replace my bad ones.

There are two things to aim at in life: first, to get what you want; and, after that, to enjoy it. Only the wisest of mankind can achieve the second.
—Logan Pearsall Smith

Through our work in the program, we are learning a new way of life. We may never achieve all we want in life, but along the way we may find ourselves enriched by our progress. Perhaps we didn't argue with our partners last week or maybe we made plans on our own or tried something new. How did we celebrate such great gains? Have we spent time enjoying the good things in our lives?

When we make any gain, we need to stop for a moment and enjoy it. No gain is too small to be recognized and enjoyed. All the time we have to enjoy our progress is right now. Let's take time to enjoy the fruits of our labors.

What gains—big or small—have I made today? Tonight I can enjoy the gains while they are fresh in my mind. I have done well.

I think the important thing is caring about someone. It's being by themselves that does people in, makes them old and bitter.
—*Thomas Tryon*

Isolation is always a choice. We choose the times we wish to be with people and the times we don't. Sometimes we choose to be alone to center ourselves—to "get away from it all." But when we start to spend too much time away from others, it's time to take a look at the reasons for our isolation.

Perhaps we're afraid to take risks with people and expose our vulnerable selves to them. Or maybe we feel people wouldn't really like us if they knew us. We may believe people will only hurt us, and we can look back into our past to recall such times.

But we are different people today. We're involved in a program based on love, trust, faith, and hope. It is a program centered on meetings filled with people caring for one another—exchanging phone numbers, hugging, getting together for coffee, listening, and understanding. It is our choice: isolation or the wonderful benefits of people caring for people.

Do I feel isolated tonight? How can I feel more connected?

I have but one lamp by which my feet are guided, and that is the lamp of experience.
—*Patrick Henry*

Think what it would be like to walk through the woods at night without a flashlight. We would be at the mercy of every root, stump, tangle, rock, and hole. Though we may have walked the same way in daylight, without the guidance of light it is as if we are walking the path for the first time.

Experience teaches us to use tools when necessary. If something didn't work for us once, it is up to us to keep trying until we find something that will work.

Why stumble in the dark agony of fear, sadness, doubt, anxiety, and insecurity? We have many flashlights to light our paths. They are the slogans, such as *Let Go and Let God, First Things First,* and *Easy Does It.* Our experiences and those of others tell us the program works. We can choose to stumble in the dark or walk easily with the light of the program.

Although I may be feeling low tonight, I can trust in the experience that tells me to let go, for all is well.

*Everything that is in agreement with our
personal desires seems true. Everything that is
not puts us into a rage.*

—Andre Maurois

There was a woman who prided herself on her ability to achieve. In fact, she bought a button that read: "I want it all—I want the best—and I want it now!" Most of the time she got what she wanted, and that made her very happy. But when she didn't get what she wanted, she would throw temper tantrums. We may be like that woman. It may be difficult to accept less than we desire. Not getting our way may be cause for battle, and we may not give up our fight until we do get our way.

If everyone acted this way, what would the world be like? Not everyone can be a "taker," receiving all the time. And not everyone can be a "giver," giving all the time. Giving once doesn't mean we always have to give, just as receiving once doesn't mean we'll always receive. We need to keep in mind that there is a balance. To achieve that balance, we need to learn we cannot have everything we want. And that's okay.

Do I fly into a rage when I don't get my own way? Help me learn how to receive, as well as how to give.

Lost, yesterday, somewhere between sunrise and sunset, two golden hours, each set with sixty diamond minutes. No reward is offered, for they are gone forever.

—Horace Mann

As we reflect on the day, were there moments we wasted? Was there a chunk of time we idled away, perhaps bored or listless? Those moments are gone now. We can never get them back, but we can be more conscious about wasting time tomorrow.

When we were drinking or using, we probably wasted a lot of time in bars, in front of the television, or passed out. We may have argued constantly with our drunken spouses or parents, wasting precious evenings and weekends. Or we may have spent all our time with our family and not any time with friends.

We don't have to waste time. We can give to others, but not to the extent that it infringes upon our time. We can walk away from an argument and venture out on evenings and weekends. We can put away the bottles and the pills and go to meetings and experience life sober and clean. Time we've wasted is gone, but the time to come we can use. We can let every minute count.

I won't waste any more of my life. I will make the most of every minute and resolve not to let precious time slip away.

The first step in solving a problem is to tell someone about it.

—John Peter Flynn

Many times we may believe we should keep our problems to ourselves. Why should we worry others? Or perhaps we don't believe we'll get help and support, only pity and sympathy. Maybe we don't want others to know we have problems.

Everybody has problems, even the people who seem to be all smiles and good cheer. Yet nobody solves problems alone. Many call upon their Higher Power or a close friend. Others use their sponsor or counselor. Some use meetings. All of these people who share their problems will find a solution. It's when we don't use any other sources that our problems become too difficult to handle.

Every problem has a solution, but that answer may not lie within our grasp. When we ask for answers, we are admitting we can't find the answers ourselves. That is the First Step to the program and the first step to living sanely and sensibly. A shared problem is always a solved problem.

I can share my problems with my Higher Power tonight. I can ask for help and thereby find a solution.

The voice of intelligence is soft and weak. It is drowned out by the roar of fear. It is ignored by the voice of desire. It is contradicted by the voice of shame. It is hissed away by hate and extinguished by anger. Most of all, it is silenced by ignorance.

—Karl Menninger

The story of Sybil tells of a woman who sheltered sixteen personalities within her. Her confusion and fear about the many voices made it almost impossible to make decisions and to be herself. Instead of being one person she was sixteen, until she got help.

Many times we may feel like Sybil. Inside, many voices try to tell us what to do, contradict us, knock us down, or make us cringe in fear. Yet we don't have to listen to those voices. We only need listen to the one that is guided by our Higher Power. That voice tells us we're good, we're doing good things for ourselves, and the program gives us all we need to get better. This voice can become louder and more powerful in time, gradually drowning out the other voices we've let run our lives.

Tonight I'll tune in the best voice—the one of my Higher Power. I'll turn my will over to this voice and let it guide me.

JUNE

As the old man walked the beach at dawn, he noticed a young man ahead of him picking up starfish and flinging them into the sea. Finally catching up with the youth, he asked him why he was doing this. The answer was that the stranded starfish would die if left until the morning sun. "But the beach goes on for miles and there are millions of starfish," countered the other. "How can your effort make any difference?" The young man looked at the starfish in his hand and then threw it to safety in the waves. "It makes a difference to this one," he said.

—Minnesota Literacy Council

Our efforts can make a difference. There will be many starfish on the paths we will travel and how we treat them will make a difference in our growth. The best resolution we can make tonight is to pay attention to the starfish we'll see. If we can reach out to all who need us, we will have made a difference to their lives and to ours.

My efforts can make a difference. I can take the first step toward making changes, taking risks, expressing feelings, and letting in the positive feelings of life.

You're only human, you're supposed to make mistakes.

—Billy Joel

Are we determined faultfinders? It may be easy for us to point fingers at others or to cite instances of wrongdoing. It may also be easy for us to misinterpret another's actions, twist words, or make something seem totally opposite to the truth.

Everyone makes mistakes, including us. But somewhere along the path of our growth, we learned we could defend ourselves if we were judge and jury. So we took a defensive stance, clinging to our battle stations as we weathered school, family, relationships, and careers.

We don't have to be so ready to make ourselves blameless and faultless. We can disband our courts of law at any time. But when we do, we will be admitting to ourselves and the people in our lives that we are only human. When we, too, can see ourselves as human, we'll no longer look at life as a battlefield, but as a classroom where everyone is both teacher and student.

I can see myself as human and accept that no human being is blameless.

The ebb and flow of will is like the movements of the tides. . . . If we cease our vain struggles and lamentations long enough to look away from the personal self . . . we realize life is going well with us after all.
—*Charles B. Newcomb*

Everything in nature changes. We can trust the sun and moon will rise and set, the tide will ebb and flow, and the seasons will change. Because we can trust these things to happen, we can learn to trust the fact that extremes in nature are normal.

So it is with people. We laugh and cry, work and play, we are young and we grow old. There will be extremes with us, just as there are in nature. And as nature finds its natural flow even after the worst disasters, so can we find our natural flow.

There is a rhythm in life that leads us to awaken and one that guides us to sleep. Tonight our natural rhythm will lead us to peace and relaxation. If we can flow with that rhythm, we'll give the quiet calmness a chance to revitalize us for tomorrow. Now is the time to follow nature's rhythm and sleep in peace.

Can I rest tonight in quietness of mind, soul, and body and trust I will find my natural flow?

In three words, I can sum up everything I've learned about life: It goes on.
—*Robert Frost*

If we've ever dug in a garden and unearthed an ants' nest, we can recall their first reaction to our unintended destruction: they do everything possible to save their lives and supplies. The ants scurry around, moving the larvae to an underground room. Exposed contents are then relocated to unseen passages. In a matter of minutes, the ants are again safely underground and ready to resume their daily routines.

How do we react when some catastrophe or unplanned event occurs? Do we want to crawl under a rock or are we as resilient as the ants? Instead of moaning over postponed plans or the loss of something in our lives, we can try to be like the ants and learn how to best work *with* circumstances that come our way.

Life doesn't stop for us to lick wounds or add fuel to grievances. Hours pass, we grow older, nature continues. Every event is part of life's cycle. We can't run away from anything. We must meet life head-on and adjust to its ebb and flow.

I can look at an unplanned event in my life as part of life's cycle. I need to trust that life will go on.

Fear imprisons, faith liberates; fear paralyzes, faith empowers; fear disheartens, faith encourages; fear sickens, faith heals; fear makes useless, faith makes serviceable.
—*Harry Emerson Fosdick*

It has been said that the opposite of fear is faith. But how do we change our fears into faith if we have little or no faith? How do we start having faith? One of the easiest ways to develop an alternative to fear is to ask ourselves during a moment of fear: What is the worst that could happen? Once we know the answer to that question, we have dealt with the source of our fears—the unknown.

What do we fear now? First we need to identify all the unknowns that we fear. Once we recognize all the things that can happen, we will be able to prepare ourselves for possible failure, loss, or sadness. By recognizing the fears, we take away some of their power over us. We can then believe we will be all right.

What do I fear and why do I fear it? I know I am okay because I have identified my fear.

Mankind has advanced in the footsteps of men and women of unshakable faith. Many of these great ones . . . have set stars in the heavens to light others through the night.
—Olga Rosmanith

All around us there are wonderful role models. Their faith, hope, strength, courage, and fearlessness can give us guidance during any time of need. But in order to look to those people for inspiration, we first need to be ready to look beyond ourselves.

In our times of need, it's easy to focus solely on ourselves. It's almost as if we climb into our own womb, conscious only of our feelings, thoughts, pains, and needs.

Yet there are those among us who have lived through times just as trying as the ones we're in. However, instead of looking inward, these people looked outward to the solutions and applied them. By using the same solutions, we can bring some light into our darkness.

Where can I find my powers of example?

The mind is its own place, and in itself—Can make a heaven of hell, a hell of heaven.
—John Milton

If we listen to the news, we can hear stories of natural disasters, starvation and deprivation, torture and bloodshed. Yet we may sit in our homes and look at our lives and moan, "Life isn't fair to me. Nothing ever works out the way I want it to."

If we could lose our self-centeredness and look at the powerlessness issues that go on outside of our little world, we would realize our hell is of its own creation. When we see what we don't have and what we can't change, we are building the foundations of a hell memorial. We are striving to preserve the have-nots and are-nots as a fitting tribute to all we cannot be.

We can stop eulogizing such negativity. Sure, there are many bad things in this world and a lot of bad people. Sure, there are many things we cannot do and possibly never will be able to do. But we can tear down the tribute to hell and erect instead a tribute to heaven—to all the things we can have and can do, to all the things we can change.

I can build tributes to my life, not memorials. The Serenity Prayer can help me see blessings, not bitterness tonight.

We ought to hear at least one little song every day, read a good poem, see a first-rate painting, and if possible speak a few sensible words.
—*Johann Wolfgang Von Goethe*

Schedules! At the end of a day, have we ever felt we've accomplished anything? Maybe we did everything according to our schedules, but were we able to take time to do the things we wanted?

Dinner doesn't have to be eaten at a fixed hour. Work doesn't have to be brought home every night. Chores don't have to be done on the same night every week. A little variation in our evening schedules is healthy, especially if we need a change of pace. It will also help us unwind, center ourselves, be more alert and in touch with life rather than frantically trying to keep pace.

Read a book. Play a record that's been collecting dust. Call a friend. Write a letter. Go for a walk. Prepare a special dessert. Take a hot, luxurious bath. We can break the weekly routine and add a new one—pampering ourselves.

What can I do special for me? I can decide tonight what I'd really like to do—and then tomorrow, I'll do it!

When you worry, you go over the same ground endlessly and come out the same place you started. Thinking makes progress from one place to another. . . . The problem of life is to change worry into thinking and anxiety into creative action.

—Harold B. Walker

The prisoner in a narrow jail cell has one path to pace—walking the same path with the same amount of paces at the same rate. It never changes until that prisoner is released.

When we worry, we are like that prisoner. Worry keeps our minds confined to one set of thoughts and keeps our physical bodies in a state of anxiety. We may believe that by thinking of the problem, we are working on a resolution. But we are really only dwelling on the futility of the problem.

It is only when we are released from worry that we can see solutions clearly. Tonight, let us free ourselves from worry's constraints, change our minds from tunnel vision to clear thoughts. These thoughts are the key to our release from worry and anxiety.

I don't have to stay prisoner to worrisome thoughts. Tonight I can allow clear thinking to give me freedom from worry.

I wish there were windows to my soul, so that you could see some of my feelings.
　　　　　　　　　　　　　　—Artemus Ward

Wouldn't it be great if people could see our feelings? All we'd have to do is walk into a room and someone could say, "I see you're feeling sad right now. Let me help you."

Many of us grew up expecting people to be mind readers. Without voicing our feelings or asking for help, we believed people should be able to see how we felt. When they didn't, we usually became angry, hurt, or depressed. Until someone pointed this out to us, we never recognized how silent we were and how great our expectations were of others.

Unless we voice our feelings, they will never be heard. And unless we ask for help, we will never get assistance. The people in our lives have ears to listen and arms to hold us—if we choose to open the windows to our soul.

I can tell someone how I feel. I can ask for help if I need it. If those around me seem to be upset, I can be there for them but I will not try to be a mind reader.

So I can't sink down and let the time of my real being take me, for if I try and for a moment can see no direction, cannot tell where I am going, I am filled with panic, scared of emptiness. I must be doing something. . . .

—Joanna Field

Imagine for a moment that we have no plans for tomorrow. No job to get up for or classes to attend, no errands to run. At first we may think this is delightful, but we need to think back to the last occasion we had time to spend alone.

Did we sit comfortably, clearing our minds of all thought and tension to listen to our inner selves? Or did we immediately turn on the television, reach for a book, or aimlessly putter?

We may be afraid to sit alone in our stillness. Yet when we allow our inner selves to be heard without background noise or the diversions of projects or hobbies, we will begin to discover our inner thoughts are creative and stimulating and intuitive. We will begin to discover ourselves.

Tonight I can take fifteen minutes to lie quietly with myself. If I have to ask what I will think about, I know I can Let Go and Let God.

Use what talents you have; the woods would have little music if no birds sang their song except those who sang best.
—Rev. Oliver G. Wilson

The perfectionist in all of us gives us some pretty harsh criticism. It tells the photographer in us we'll never be Ansel Adams. It tells the writer in us we'll never be Charles Dickens. It tells the businessperson in us we'll never be Henry Ford. It tells the parent in us we'll never have the perfect family.

This perfectionist has an uncanny way of making us feel inferior to all who have gone before us. Such condemnations may hurt our creativity and abilities so much that we decide to give up trying to be good at anything. So we fail before we begin.

How do we know we won't be good at what we do? We certainly won't be Ansel Adams or anybody else because they've already existed. But we can be ourselves and use our talents to do our best. We may become famous and successful, or we may not. But we won't know unless we try. With our talents and determination, we can achieve splendid things. But we won't know unless we try.

What are my talents? I can develop these talents not in imitation of another but with curiosity about what I can do.

*This time, like all times, is a very good one if we
but know what to do with it.*
—Ralph Waldo Emerson

Is the glass half full or half empty? We know the answer to that question can symbolically reflect whether we have a positive or negative outlook on life. If we see the glass as half empty, we focus on what is gone. But if we say the glass is half full, we see what remains.

If we're full of ideas about how to spend our time, then our outlook is positive and we'll not waste a second. But if we're feeling bored or directionless or lonely, our days may be filled with a lot of negative energy and wasted moments.

Instead of focusing on what we don't have, we can change our attitude and look at what we do have. We have choices about how we want to spend our time. The decisions we make will have a direct bearing on how meaningful each day will be.

How can I change my attitude and make each day full?

A father who cares enough to wait and worry,
who cares enough to counsel and be concerned,
is among the greatest blessings God has given.
—*Richard L. Evans*

The memories we have of our childhood may be filled with joy, sorrow, happiness, or pain. The child within us may still be crying for a father with whom to share our joys and growth. We may feel cheated out of a wonderful relationship with him or saddened because that relationship has ended.

A loving, healthy father is a great blessing. Yet many of us do not have such a blessing. Instead of thinking back to childhood with feelings of anger or bitterness, we each need to believe our father did the best he could to raise us. Our father had to deal with his imperfections and circumstances at the same time he was also trying to be a father to us.

We can look back and remember the good things about our father. By looking at the good along with the bad, we'll see him as human instead of imperfect.

I need to see my father as another human sharing my path in life. Can I see the good in him?

I wish to live without hate, whim, jealousy, envy, fear. I wish to be simple, honest, frank, natural, clean in mind and clean in body . . . to face any obstacle and meet every difficulty unabashed and unafraid.

—Elbert Hubbard

Growing up, we learned there were many places to make wishes: the first star, a well, candles on a birthday cake. We saw Dorothy return from Oz after she wished she were back home. Fairy tales taught us wishes can come true.

We don't have to stop wishing, even though many of our wishes never came true. We may have wished for the impossible when we said: "I wish things would get better at home." But we may have gotten our way when we said: "I wish this pain would end." Our dreams came true with the program.

Our best wishes can be about ourselves and the lives we want to have. We can wish for riches and find friends with hearts of gold. We can wish for comfort and health, and get a night of uninterrupted sleep. Whatever we wish for, we can receive.

I can read tonight's quotation aloud and apply it to my life. This powerful affirmation can help me tonight and every night.

Love comes unseen; we only see it go.
          —*Austin Dobson*

How often are we blind to love shown us by others? Yet we are always aware when love is taken from us. Suddenly we feel helpless, alone, rejected, and full of despair. "No one will ever love me again!" we may cry. Yet all around us are loving people, ready to give their support.

If we only equate love with a sexual relationship, we will never see love's beauty. Love comes in so many forms and from so many people. When we experience the loss of a love, we may believe we have lost all the love that will ever be shown to us.

Love is more than Valentine's Day and passion and giddy feelings of ecstasy. When we desire love in that form, we are like addicts craving a drug. The effects are blissful, but they are only temporary. Love that lasts, that stays with patience and strength, is the love that binds all of humanity. It is what makes us smile at a stranger, it's what makes long-term friendships, it's what makes us feel pain, as well as joy. Love is the connection we have with every person in our lives.

Tonight, I feel the love I have for others and the love they have for me. I can learn to see the love that exists all around me.

*When you want to hurry something, that means
you no longer care about it and want to get on to
other things.*

—Robert M. Pirsig

At times we may feel pressured to accomplish certain things in a short period of time. We may find ourselves rushing through activities aimlessly, operating under some kind of invisible deadline. Or we may be looking forward to future events and wish the present would hurry up and end.

Now is the time to slow ourselves down. Like a swimmer before a race, we can take time to breathe deeply, relax our tense muscles, and test the waters before we take the plunge.

We can use *Let Go and Let God, Easy Does It,* and *Keep it Simple* as our guidelines. As we let these slogans relax us, we can get a clearer picture about the reasons for our hurrying. By examining these reasons, we can then determine what activities we really need to work on—at a much slower pace.

What slogans will help me relax my hustle-bustle pace?

*For the happiest life, days should be rigorously
planned, nights left open to chance.*
　　　　　　　　　　　　—Mignon McLaughlin

How spontaneous are we? Are we more rigid people
or more flexible? If our plans suddenly change, do we
handle that easily or is it difficult for us? If we're more
rigid, change is often difficult for us to deal with. We
may feel anger, resentment, hurt, or sadness when a
friend calls to cancel an engagement or something
happens to interrupt our plans. We may find ourselves so rigid that we have difficulty going to a meeting and parking in a different space or sitting in a
different seat.

Rigidity is built over time and so must be loosened
up with time. Little changes in our patterns will help
us deal with little changes in our lives. By gradually
learning to accept smaller changes, we'll learn to deal
with bigger ones. To become more flexible on a daily
basis, we need to make slow and gentle changes. Over
time, we'll learn to change from rigidity to spontaneity
and flexibility.

---

*I can make a small change in tomorrow's schedule. Each
day I'll make a minor change to help develop flexibility.*

The man who makes no mistakes lacks boldness and the spirit of adventure. He never tries anything new. He is a brake on the wheels of progress.

—M. W. Larmour

"Progress, not perfection" is all the program asks of us. Yet our expectations to do everything the right way at the right time—and usually without asking for help—only lead to incredible disappointment and a sense of failure.

When Henry Ford made his first automobile, he forgot to make a reverse gear. Was that a failure? Not if we look at how his next car—the Model T—revolutionized the automobile industry. Ford learned from his mistake and used that knowledge to build something even better.

Tonight we're building something even better—ourselves. But we won't be able to make a perfect model, only a better one. To do so, we need to accept the fact that we're going to make mistakes along the way.

What mistakes have I made today that I can learn from tonight?

Hope is the only bee that makes honey without flowers.

—Robert Ingersoll

Hope is the invisible part of ourselves that can be the difference between getting somewhere and getting nowhere. Hope is the extra set of muscles that allows us to carry on even though our legs can't support us any longer. Hope is the extra heartbeat that gives us positive energy when our senses can't feel, hear, or see beyond negativity. Hope is the nectar that restores health when our bodies feel old and broken-down.

The one thing everyone in the program has is hope. Hope keeps us sane and keeps us trying. For as long as we have hope, we'll always feel a candle burning within us that's ready to light the world.

We increase our supply of hope every time we do something good, even when we don't want to. Hope is the extra push we give ourselves to quench rage, to bolster our reserves of patience, and to feel love when we find it difficult to feel. With hope in our lives, all else is possible.

Do I have hope tonight? Help me remain filled with hope about my life and the lives of those around me.

A person remains immature, whatever his age, as long as he thinks of himself as an exception to the human race.

—Harry A. Overstreet

Most every rule has an exception because of special people or circumstances. We may sometimes believe we are exceptions to the rule when it comes to the program. We may believe our set of circumstances or who we are makes us different. We may feel the slogans and Steps are good for most people, but they don't relate to us because of some unique things we believe no one else has.

Even though each of us is a unique individual with our own lifestyles and set of circumstances, we're no different than anyone else in the program. We are in the program for one purpose: To learn to live a better way of life while coping with the effects of an addiction. Once we realize we're working toward the same solution as everyone else, we won't see ourselves as exceptions. Our growth will occur in leaps and bounds once we're freed from the label of "exception to the rule."

I'm no different than anyone else when I look at the reasons why I'm in the program. I will remember my connection, not my exception.

One must do more, think less, and not watch oneself live.
—*Sebastien Roch Nicolas de Chamfort*

A talk show host was interviewing a new starlet. Every time he asked her a question she watched herself in the monitor, listening more to herself than to him. Midway through the show, she was totally flustered trying to watch herself and keep up with the show's progress.

At times we may be so focused on ourselves that we are unable to see anyone else. We soon become our own greatest fans, watching only ourselves and listening only to our own thoughts. Reflecting on today, we may be conscious of how much time we spent talking about ourselves or focusing attention on ourselves and our issues.

We can start to change this behavior. Instead of spending a few hours focused on us, we can focus on a hobby, a book, a movie, or a family member. We aren't so important that we need to keep a constant watch over ourselves. There are a lot more important and more interesting people, places, and things to see.

I can stop watching myself and start noticing others. Higher Power, help me discover the world around me.

Life is like a ten-speed bike. Most of us have gears we never use.
—*Charles M. Schulz*

To ride a ten-speed bike, we need to learn to use the gears. If we're going uphill, we should know what gear eases the climb. If we're going downhill, we should know what gear best uses the slope of the hill.

The Twelve Steps of the program are like the bicycle gears. If we know the purpose and benefit of each Step, we can use them to ease our way. Sometimes life may feel like an uphill climb. Steps Two and Three teach us to call on our Higher Power for help. If we're contentedly coasting on a wonderful slope, then others may benefit from our strength and hope if we use Step Twelve. If we're struggling to change our behaviors or character defects, then Steps Four, Five, and Six may ease our struggles.

If we use all the Steps when we need them, we will never have to struggle again. But if we ignore them like never-used gears, they will become rusty and unproductive. Proper maintenance means we must use everything frequently in order to get the best benefit. We must use the Steps as much as we can.

Do I need to study the Steps more so I can use them better?

Don't find fault. Find a remedy.

—*Henry Ford*

A person in need and a listener were on the telephone. "The problem is," began the one in need, "I wouldn't be in this situation if those things hadn't happened." The one in need talked on, listing all the people, places, and things that brought him to such a state.

The listener let him finish, and then replied, "I believe you're blaming people, places, and things for your problems. You can only blame yourself because you're the one who can change things. As long as you hide behind 'causes' you won't take action. It's up to you to act, so do it!"

It may be easier to blame, because finding remedies means we'll have to work. Looking for scapegoats for our current situation won't get us out of our ruts, it will only mire us deeper. To get free, we need to use our talents and wisdom to good benefit. As the listener said, it's up to us to take action, so let's do it!

Tonight I can stop finding scapegoats. It's up to me to find remedies for my current position and to help pull me out of a rut. Let me do it!

Blame yourself if you have no branches or leaves; don't accuse the sun of partiality.
  —*Chinese proverb*

How much do we use our past to find reasons for our faults or shortcomings today? Because we may have come from alcoholic homes or impoverished households doesn't give us the license to place blame for the way we are.

We may feel we would be easier to get along with if other people didn't act the way they did. We may believe we would have so many more hours in the day if others didn't take up so much of our valuable time.

If one tree in a forest is thirsty and starved for sunlight, it doesn't blame the other trees around it for drinking its water and basking in its sun. If the tree wants water it spreads its roots wider and deeper to seek water. If it wants sunlight it spreads its branches and reaches higher. Like that tree in the forest, so must we concentrate on the things we need to do for our nourishment and growth. Our health depends on ourselves, not upon the failings of those around us.

I can look at my growth, and do the things I need for me.

It's better to be a lion for a day than a sheep all your life.
—*Sister Elizabeth Kenny*

Following the crowd, going along with the majority, or doing for the approval of others makes us like sheep. Sheep travel in packs behind a leader or are guided by the barks and nips of sheepdogs. Sheep never travel alone and one sheep never leads the others. Are we like sheep?

By following the norm, we've learned life may be easier without arguments or disagreements over bucking the trend. But how has such following helped us grow? Do we really know who we are, or are we more aware of how everyone else is?

To walk against the wind once in a while is healthy. We don't always have to follow the crowd if we don't believe the crowd is right. We can be like a lion once in a while: a leader, unafraid to travel alone or to guide others. We can let out a mighty roar that will set us apart from the din of the crowd. We don't have to be sheep all the time, only when we want to be.

Will I be a leader or a follower? Whichever I choose, let me believe my choice is the best for me.

If we want to keep living with ourselves, we must keep on trying, trying, trying.
                              —*Robert J. White, M.D.*

Tonight we may feel we failed in some way today. Even though we may have done our best, we may now believe we could have done more, done it better, or tried harder, then things would be different now.

But there are things beyond our control. One of them is the outcome of any circumstance. We cannot expect that, if we do all we can, all will be well. Even the most skilled surgeon loses patients. The surgeon knows the grace of God is with the patient, no matter what the outcome.

The grace of God is in our lives and the lives of those around us. Though we strive to do our best and to make everything better, we need to remember the outcomes are not in our control. How we accept them, however, is in our control.

Higher Power, help me keep trying to do my best, no matter what the outcome.

Anger blows out the lamp of the mind
—*Robert Green Ingersoll*

When we feel anger, our hearts pound faster and we feel warmer. We can go through our daily motions and from the outside look as if all was well. But under the surface is a pot of boiling anger that we keep stoked throughout the day.

Remaining angry for more than a few minutes can be as dangerous as letting a cancerous growth go untreated. It will overtake our healthy thoughts and bodies until we become emotionally and physically sick. We'll become sicker the longer we let anger run our mental, spiritual, and physical selves.

The time to deal with anger is the moment we feel it, not later. If we can't confront the source of our anger at the moment, we still need to let go of it. Getting out our anger doesn't necessarily mean yelling, throwing things, or setting ultimatums. Letting our anger go means letting it be felt and expressed, then releasing it. Anger with obsession makes us sick; anger with expression keeps us sane and healthy.

Am I holding on to anger from the past? I can let go of this anger tonight and not let it rule me.

If you can't be thankful for what you receive, be thankful for what you escape.

—*Anonymous*

Those Jews who were fortunate enough to evade the clutches of the Third Reich were extremely grateful for their escape from family separations, torture, and death. Even though they may have fled their homes, possessions, friends, and businesses, and had little food in their stomachs, they could give thanks for what they did have: their lives and hope for a better future.

How thankful are we for what we have? Many times we aren't grateful for the shirts on our backs and food in our stomachs. We criticize our lives and our family, perhaps even ourselves. We find we aren't happy, healthy, mature, or serene enough. But imagine for a moment what it was like in our pre-recovery days.

Remember pain, sickness, confusion, anger, hopelessness? We've escaped from the bleakness of the past. But if we can't be grateful for the good in our lives tonight, we've not learned a thing from the program. To be grateful for our new path of discovery, all we need to do is look back at the rocky road we used to travel.

Tonight I can be grateful for what I've gained and what is gone.

Victory is not won in miles, but in inches. Win a little now, hold your ground, and later win a little more.

—Louis L'Amour

For athletes to succeed as runners, they must not stop after their first race is won. To become the best, they need constant practice and warm-ups, and race after race. Some races they will win; others they won't. But in each race they will have achieved another step in their success as a runner.

We, too, must set goals and achieve them step by step. When we entered the program, our goal may have been to know ourselves well enough to make decisions. We then entered "little races" that led toward that goal: sharing our feelings, asking for help, taking our Fourth Step, telling a friend what we wanted to do. Each time we accomplished one, we moved closer to our goal.

We need to give ourselves credit for all the "little races" we've won. If we look not to the goal but to the path, we will see we are gaining ground step by step.

I can take another step toward my goals. Each small step deserves recognition and praise.

JULY

Why do some people always see beautiful skies and grass and lovely flowers and incredible human beings, while others are hard-pressed to find anything or any place that is beautiful?
—Leo Buscaglia

We may have some pretty strong feelings about those people who come to meetings and say only positive things. We may feel uncomfortable with their smiling faces and warm welcomes. We may wonder how anyone could be so happy. We know they wouldn't be happy if they had a day like we had today!

It's hard to break the pattern of seeing only the negative things. We've spent so long at the bottom of the barrel that it's hard to be at the top. It takes work to think of things in a positive way; that may be a new way of thinking for us.

But we can start thinking positively. Instead of remembering all the negative things that happened today, we can sift through until we find just one positive thing. After a while we may come up with two, or three, or many more. Soon, we may be one of those positive people with a cheery outlook!

Can I think of one positive thing that happened to me today? Can I express this positive thing to others?

*When we stop looking at whatever troubles us,
and turn in faith to God, the source of good, the
difficulty disappears and a new condition takes
its place.*

—*William A. Clough*

If our garden is choked with weeds, we don't stare
at it and think, "My garden is going to have a lousy
growing season." We start pulling those weeds to give
our plants room to grow and the nutrition they need.
Because we believe clearing the weeds will make the
garden grow, we change a bad condition into a good
one.

But what do we do when we see ourselves being
choked by debts, bad relationships, or health problems? Do we take action to affect change or do we become paralyzed at our view of an unchangeable
situation? We need to learn to take our focus off fears,
doubts, worries, and insecurities and place it instead
upon faith and a belief that all will work out.

We can begin to replace difficulties with faith. No
matter what problems we have, none is too big for
faith to change. Our belief that these conditions can
change is the first step in letting faith work its own
way.

*Tonight I can change my outlook by replacing my
difficulties with faith.*

We can't all be captains, we've got to be crew.
—*Douglas Malloch*

An old saying tells us, *There is no I in* team. That means there is no one hero, no one member who carries a team or becomes the personality of the team. The team wins or loses because of all its members, not the actions or omissions of one.

There are many of us who don't like to play on a team. We would prefer individual sports or hobbies. We may like to be in control or seek solitude rather than the company of others. We may even try to assume so many responsibilities that we become the only person who can accomplish a task or job.

Sometimes it's good to be a leader. But leaders also need to know how to be led. To work well with other people, we need to know what it feels like to be a member of a group where we are all equal. A ship comprised of only captains may flounder or be tossed against the shore. A ship with one captain and a crew may sail smoothly and safely by the efforts of all.

Let me become a member of my group, not a leader. Help me extend this affirmation into all areas of my life.

Silence propagates itself, and the longer talk has been suspended, the more difficult it is to find anything to say.

—Samuel Johnson

Remember growing up with a parent or other family member who showed anger by "the silent treatment"? How infuriating it was to experience this. One person would be attempting to make things right or provoke a response while the other would maintain a "lips sealed" policy.

Forced silence can be as devastating as the most angry, most vicious comment. Forced silence is a wall erected in front of the vocal chords so human communication cannot scale it.

The silent treatment, like inappropriate anger, is not the way to patch rips in the fabric of our human support system. Unless we break the soundless barrier, the wall will become nearly impossible to tear down. Tonight we can look back to any relationship that's in jeopardy and seek to mend it by human communication.

Is there someone in my life with whom I haven't communicated for a while? It's up to me to scale the wall of silence before I lose that person forever.

Patience is a virtue that carries a lot of WAIT!
—Our Daily Bread

Before we came into the program, we may have had little patience. We may have been tired of waiting for our parents to sober up and live up to their promises. We may have impatiently crossed off the days until we were legally free to leave home.

When we entered the program, we again found we had to wait for so many things. We learned the Twelve Steps couldn't be done in twelve days. We listened to people talk about the years of recovery they had. We may have privately thought it wouldn't take us that long. We were going to be in and out of the program in a matter of weeks—and we would be cured!

Good things come to those who wait could be another program slogan because it is so true. To truly master any skill requires long hours of study and continual practice. Like playing the piano, we start out with short, easy chords that build to full-length concertos. Our goal in the program is to play concertos for the rest of our lives. That will not happen today, nor tomorrow, but will come in time.

I can use what I've learned in the program to begin my lifelong study. Higher Power, help me have patience.

Panics, in some cases, have their uses. Their duration is always short; the mind soon grows through them and acquires a firmer habit than before.

—Thomas Paine

Any anxious feeling is a signal that needs attention. It means there's something going on, and it's a way our bodies communicate that they are being overwhelmed. If we ask ourselves what's going on, we might hear answers of frustration, shame, guilt, or fear over things that are over and done with or things that have yet to occur.

One of the ways to get through an attack is to center ourselves in the present. We can do this by remembering the date, time, and temperature. Then we can identify objects around us, including what we're wearing. This exercise will bring us back into the present where we won't have the feelings that contributed to our attacks. When our minds are clear, we can learn from anxiety and grow through it.

Tonight I can keep myself in the present by identifying the things and people around me that exist for this moment.

You have learned something. That always feels at first as if you had lost something.
—*George Bernard Shaw*

We listen as we watch the newcomer cry, "After coming to meetings, I realized my parents couldn't be there for me anymore. They have an addictive disease and I can't get the help I need from them. I feel like I've lost them!" We may nod our heads as we relate these words to our lives.

Didn't we feel like we had lost family, friends, or mates when we began learning the truths in the program? As we learned about addiction, we were faced with just how much we had depended on others to help us. We discovered we weren't who we thought we were. We realized there could be another way of life.

A snake must shed its old skin before the new one can appear. Like furniture, parts of us become worn and uncomfortable. We must replace the old with the new. For every gain, there must be a loss. But instead of mourning our losses tonight, we can rejoice over what we have gained.

I can be grateful for all the gains in my life and in my growth. The losses have allowed me to become stronger and more fruitful.

When we are tired, we are attacked by ideas we conquered long ago.
        —*Friedrich Wilhelm Nietzsche*

Many times our late night thinking is like a late night movie. It can be scary, it's usually of poor quality, and it makes little sense. Trying to understand ourselves or to make decisions during such times only leads to crazy thoughts.

When we can't apply the Steps and the principles of the program because our minds are running like a late night movie, we have only one alternative to insanity. That's to go to bed. Shut off the movie reel and go to sleep. When our bodies are tired, our muscles can't perform and we're left with little energy. This kind of thinking is our mind's only way of telling us that it needs rest. We need to respect this.

The program works for us when we're alert, focused, and able to process healthy thinking. Tired minds breed tired thoughts—thoughts we've been over many times. The cure for a tired mind is an alert one, and the medicine is a good night's sleep!

Tonight I can shut off the late night movie reels of my mind and go to sleep. Sleep is my Higher Power's gift to help my mind get the rest it needs.

You take yourself too seriously! You are too damn important in your own mind. That must be changed!

—Carlos Castaneda

How can we appreciate the world around us if we're blinded by our self-importance? Like the horse who wears blinders, we only see ourselves apart from everything else. We miss the natural beauty and the loveliness of human nature if we only have a mirror before our eyes.

Losing self-importance begins by opening our eyes and ears to those around us. By listening to others, we learn our lives and experiences are not unique. By looking around us, we see we have the same good qualities—and bad traits—as others.

Today may have been a day when we were blinded by our own self-importance. Yet tonight we can remember we are no better—and no worse—than anyone else. Tonight we can take off our blinders and become part of the world around us.

What uniqueness can I recall in the people around me today?

You must travel the river, live on it, follow it when there is morning light, and follow it when there is nothing but dark and the banks have blurred into shadows.

—Wil Haygood

Any lifeguard knows a swimmer who tries to swim against the current stands a good chance of becoming tired and drowning. *Go with the flow* is a good reminder to help us stop going against the current of life.

Tonight we may discover that our weariness is a result of swimming against today's current. We may have tried to force changes in people, places, or things. We may have even tried to force ourselves to do things we were incapable of doing.

Going with the flow tonight means accepting the way we feel—right now. It means listening to our inner voices when they tell us whether we're tired, hungry, cold, or lonely. By accepting ourselves and not fighting how we feel, we'll be better able to travel the river tonight.

Tonight I will respect myself and go with the flow.

*I never make the mistake of arguing with people
for whose opinions I have no respect.*

—*Gibbon*

"She just doesn't understand." "He doesn't listen to
me." "She can't see my point of view." Do we ever say
these things? No matter how much we argue or how
convincing our argument, we may never be able to
change another's opinion.

It may be our parents. But do we value their opinion, or are we trying to force their approval? It may be
a boss or co-worker. But are they people we would
choose to have as friends outside work? Before we become tense and angry, we must look at the person
with whom we are arguing.

Do we respect these people? Would their opinion
benefit us? Are they interested in our best welfare?
Sometimes we may struggle to change the opinion of
those who have never supported us, rather than talk
with those who have always been there for us. To dis-
tinguish between the two is the difference between
disapproval and tension, and love and acceptance.

*Am I driving myself crazy trying to change another's
opinion? I can take a look at this and seek those opinions I
value and trust.*

The highest compact we can make with our fellow is, let there be truth between us two forevermore.

—*Ralph Waldo Emerson*

When was the last time we told a lie? Do we remember who we lied to and the reason? Did our lying bring us closer to that person, or did it build an invisible wall?

We have chosen to travel on the path of recovery. Because of this, there are certain requirements for our growth and learning. One of them is honesty with ourselves and with others. If we aren't honest with ourselves, we will suffer because the truth will come out. If we aren't honest with others, we will hinder our ability to grow closer to people. Dishonesty doesn't make bonds, it breaks them.

We can make amends for our lies. We can "come clean" to those we lied to and tear down the walls. By doing so we will move further along our path of recovery by learning how to build relationships, not break them. Honesty with others builds trust, trust builds love, and love makes life so much better.

Tonight I will promise to get honest with at least one person to whom I have lied. I will learn how to build a better relationship by doing so.

There is a divine plan of good at work in my life.
I will let go and let it unfold.
—*Ruth P. Freedman*

There is a lesson to be learned from each person we meet. Our contact, however brief, has happened for some reason. We may feel as if we are part of a play, especially when we meet someone at a particularly meaningful time. Maybe we were laid off from work and for some reason attended a meeting in a different town and sat next to an employer looking for someone with our qualifications.

Yet we may question the meaning behind meeting those who leave us with pain and heartache. We may wonder at the lessons to be learned from those who may treat us badly. Not all the lessons are easy, nor do all our contacts feel wonderful. But there is a purpose that can be seen after the healing of time. We'll always meet new people, just as we'll always be learning. These things we can trust are in the hands of our Higher Power.

Tonight, I will trust that my life is lit by goodness and that all people and events can add to my light.

*It was like a revelation to me, taking complete
responsibility for one's own actions.*
—Cary Grant

All our lives we may have looked for someone to
take care of us. This may have begun with our parents,
then continued when we formed relationships. We
may have found life was easier when someone else
took responsibility for our finances, obligations, and
emotional health. Whenever someone left us, we may
have quickly latched onto someone new so we didn't
have to feel the burden of taking responsibility.

The program teaches us that we are the only ones
who can take care of us. After entering the program we
may feel like we're suddenly stripped bare, vulnerable
to the whole world of responsibility: bill paying, social
obligations, career decisions, health, and fitness.

We may not know all we need to know about taking responsibility for ourselves, but we're learning. Every time we do something on our own, for ourselves,
we are that much closer to responsible living.

*I can take responsibility for many parts of my life. When I
don't know how to do something, I can ask for help from
others.*

When I hear somebody sigh, "Life is hard," I am always tempted to ask, "Compared to what?"
—*Sydney J. Harris*

We've probably heard all the negative quotations about life. There was also probably a time when we believed them all. Based on the state of our lives at the time, it was probably no surprise that life was difficult and brutal.

Certainly there are many things in life that are harsh and cruel—we see such things in the paper every day. But there are some very wonderful things, too. It's just that we've been conditioned to believe the horrors instead of the wonders.

Today may have been a long, tiring, boring day. But that doesn't mean all days are long, tiring, and boring. There's much good in life that we can see if we let ourselves. We can get off our "life-is-difficult" soapbox and hear the humor, see the smiles, and feel the caring. Life may be difficult at times, but it is also quite fulfilling.

I need to feel that life is good tonight. What event happened today that I can feel good about? Who did I see today that made me feel good?

When something does not insist on being noticed,
when we aren't grabbed by the collar or struck
on the skull by a presence or an event, we take
for granted the very things that most deserve our
gratitude.

—Cynthia Ozick

Was today an ordinary day, one filled with the usual events, the same people, the same routine? If nothing unusual or out-of-the-ordinary happened, are we now feeling a little ho-hum about the day's predictable pattern?

It's easy to recognize the extraordinary events in a day—the ones that break the norm, perhaps add a challenge, or a chuckle, or a bit of chaos. We give those events recognition and tend to belittle the events in an ordinary day.

Tonight we can look back over our day and feel gratitude for every minute of it. We can remember our uneventful commute to work, for instance, and feel grateful that we drove in safety. We can recall the people, places, and things now and be grateful they were a part of our day.

Tonight, I will feel grateful for the good in the ordinary.

The world is full of people looking for spectacular happiness while they snub contentment.
—Doug Larson

Before we came into the program, our lives were like roller coaster rides. We'd either be on a downward plunge of despair or an upward lift of ecstasy. When we were on a high, it seemed as if nothing could take that feeling away from us. We kept going from high to high and began calling our highs happiness.

Today our lives aren't so dramatic, nor filled with such radical swings. Because we can't equate our happiness with those highs, we are often uncomfortable with feelings that don't include ecstasy or depression. Today we feel contentment, cheerfulness, serenity, and peace.

Just like we do with a pair of new shoes, we need to try on our new feelings. We need to wear them through our daily routines and our nightly schedules. It won't be long before they fit us well. Then, it won't feel so strange when we feel stability and gentleness. We'll soon learn these feelings have always been within our reach. We've just been too afraid to feel them.

Tonight I am grateful to be off the roller coaster. I am unafraid of the content feelings that I have.

When the cards are dealt and you pick up your hand . . . there's nothing you can do except to play it out for whatever it may be worth. And the way you play your hand is free will.
　　　　　　　　　　　　　—Jawaharlal Nehru

Playing a card game with a winning hand can be joyful. We gain confidence from the cards and play well, knowing we can be successful. But when we pick up a hand that could be a losing one, we may want to walk away from almost certain defeat.

How we play the hand we're dealt each day will determine the outcome. A hand that requires effort, determination, and skill to play well we may see as too difficult. Rather than play it, we may want to pass it to another and draw a new hand.

But we won't be given another hand tonight. We can pick up the cards and use the tools of the program to work through the difficult ones and try to change the hand into a good one. Win or lose, the best way to stay in the game is to play with what we have.

Tonight I can choose not to fold. I'll continue to face what life has given me today and work through things to the best of my ability.

Three ... are my friends: [One] that loves me, [one] that hates me, [one] that is indifferent to me. Who loves me, teaches me tenderness. Who hates me, teaches me caution. Who is indifferent to me, teaches me self-reliance.

—Ivan Panin

Not everyone is going to be a best friend. Some people will choose not to know us. Others may dislike us for whatever reason. Yet we can see these people as our friends by realizing each has something to offer.

We may be hurt when we realize not everyone likes us or wants to be our friend. But do we want to be friends with everyone? Certainly there are those we know who bore us, make us angry, or turn us off.

It's okay that everyone isn't our friend. We can learn from the one who dislikes us that there are aspects about our behaviors that some people won't like. We can learn from those who don't care to pursue a friendship that not everyone can be there for us. Such people will also help us appreciate more the special people in our lives who are unquestionably our friends.

I know I have some very special friends in my life. Tonight I can be grateful for their support.

Sickness tells us what we are.

—*Proverb*

Our lives are made up of many things that define who we are. Our salaries and savings tell how rich we are. Our clothes tell the colors and styles we like. The cars we drive show our tastes and transportation needs. Our homes reflect our family size and the type of furniture we like.

But those are outer, material reflections. We also have inner, emotional reflections that show who we are. Our feelings reflect whether we are happy or sad. Our muscles show whether we are relaxed or stressed. Our health reflects whether we're taking good care of ourselves or not.

Many of our stressful or emotional times are accurately reflected by a cold or flu, or negative thinking. The sick feeling we may have inside about things we are dealing with can erupt into outward signs of sickness. It's okay to be sick, but it's important to look at the sickness and come in touch with what may be going on inside. Our body defines us and expresses this definition in many ways. By noticing all expressions, we are that much more in touch with who we are.

Tonight I can observe myself and the things that define me

*Sometimes I found that in my happy moments I
could not believe that I had ever been miserable;
I planned for the future as if happiness were all
there was. . . .*

—Joanna Field

Wouldn't it be great if we could forget all the miserable times or, better still, never have them again?

In the past, our lives have been like a roller coaster ride. The thrill of going up was something we never wanted to end; when we went down, we never imagined we could leave such depths.

We may still have moments of unhappiness, sadness, or despair, but now we have the tools to trust those moments won't be with us for long. And we don't need to desperately clutch at happiness, joy, and serenity like we used to.

Whatever kind of day we have, we can trust that the bad day can get better and the good day will be back again.

---

*Did I have a good day or a bad one? Can I trust that today
was okay, no matter what kind of day it was?*

When wealth is lost, nothing is lost; when health is lost, something is lost; when character is lost, all is lost.

—German proverb

Imagine being in a foreign country when you suddenly discover you've lost your traveler's checks. At first you may panic and worry, but after a phone call to your bank, reimbursement will be sent. You have lost nothing.

Then imagine you've eaten a new dish that doesn't agree with you. You become so sick and weak that you're bedridden. Your ill health becomes more difficult to cope with, for you must let rest, medicine, and time restore you. For a time, you cannot sightsee and experience all the festivities of the foreign land.

Now imagine you've lost your passport and all forms of identification. To the authorities you are a nameless person who may need to be detained. You have now experienced the biggest loss of all, that of your character and self. Money can be replaced, health can be restored, but losing who you are and what you stand for cannot easily be regained. Hold fast to your self. It is richer than money and more valuable than good health.

Tonight I can hold dear who I am. I need to learn my possessions and my body are mere supports for myself.

The measure of success is not whether you have a tough problem to deal with, but whether it's the same problem you had last year.
　　　　　　　　　　　　　　　—John Foster Dulles

Have we been wanting to make changes in our relationships, our careers, our education, our behaviors? What efforts have we made? How much have we changed in the last year? Have we truly made the physical, emotional, and spiritual changes we needed? Or have we only paid lip service to those changes? There may be many things we want to alter in our lives. But unless we stop talking and start doing something, those changes won't happen.

We can start by setting a small, easily attainable goal. For example, we may wish to change our behavior of raising our voice. We might set this goal: "For the next twenty-four hours, I will not raise my voice—no matter what buttons are pushed in me or reactions I have." When that goal is achieved, then set another small goal. Breaking down each change into small, easily attainable steps is like working the program: a step-by-step, gradual process toward greater health and happiness.

I can set at least one easily attainable goal. I will share that goal with another and ask for help when I need it.

This is a delicious evening, when the whole body is one sense, and imbibes delight through every pore.

—Henry David Thoreau

Natural beauty can be spectacular. There is the bright, full moon, glowing orange or ethereal white. Perhaps we see it reflected on shimmering waters of a lake, like silver streaks on a cool, black mirror. City lights transform even the smoggiest and grayest of cities into a magical kingdom of colors. The rhythmical sound of rain on a road, cleansing the night air, lulls us into soothing sleep.

If we use our senses to their fullest, we can come closer to our Higher Power. We can open our eyes to the silhouettes of the trees and buildings around us, to the colorful lights. We can listen to bullfrogs croaking, crickets chirping, or the wind howling. Each night we can breathe deeply of the cool, clean air, almost feeling the evening on our face.

Just as our Higher Power created fall foliage, lush forests, and blue skies, so did our Higher Power create beauty in the night. It is up to us to open our senses and take it in.

I will experience the night's beauty. I can be grateful for the night as well as the day.

Anyhow, I say, the God I been praying and writing to is a man. And act just like all the other mens I know. Trifling, forgetful and lowdown.

—Alice Walker,
The Color Purple

When many of us first came into the program and heard the words "God" or "Higher Power," we may have wanted to walk out. We may have thought God a kind of heavenly scorekeeper who lived by "an eye for an eye; a tooth for a tooth." But we learned in the program that Higher Power could be any image we chose. Some of us found it easier to picture a pleasurable image when we thought of God, like a mountain stream. Some of us began conversing with an "invisible" friend. We learned any image we chose was okay, as long as we believed a Power greater than ourselves could restore our sanity.

Some of us may still have trouble with the concept of a Higher Power. If we remember we don't have to hold the negative images we grew up with, it may be easier to create a spiritual image with which we can be comfortable. Our Higher Power can be whatever or whomever we choose because it is a personal belief.

I can remember my Higher Power is my personal belief, not a religious dogma.

The seed of God is in us. Pear seeds grow into pear trees, nut seeds into nut trees, and God seeds into God.

—*Meister Eckhart*

Often we may feel critical and judgmental about our maturity or personality. When we read we have God seeds within us, we may find that difficult to believe. How can we have the God seeds within us that other people have? It may seem everyone else has more good within them than we have.

Just as we admire certain qualities about other people, so can we admire qualities about ourselves. We need to remember a good critic looks at both the good and the bad. A good critic doesn't pass judgment, but merely assembles the facts to allow others to make judgments.

The seeds that grow pear trees don't yield perfect trees. Some of the fruit is ripe and juicy; some is hard and dry; some fruit never matures. Yet the pear tree will be a good tree if it's tended with care. So it is with us. Every part of us may not be perfect, but with care we can make the best person possible from the God seed that began us.

I can be a healthy, bountiful person if I give myself plenty of care. Tonight I won't give up on me.

Never let your head hang down. Never give up and sit down and grieve. Find another way. And don't pray when it rains if you don't pray when the sun shines.

—*Sachel Paige*

When children are tired they make their feelings very clear. They just sit down and start to cry. As adults, we may sometimes feel like a child, ready to sit down and give up. But we're not tired children anymore. We're grown-ups, living with responsibilities and duties.

Instead of giving up, we need to find another way of handling responsibilities. To begin with, we can ask for help. There are others who can help with meals, family care, and household duties. We can also rearrange our schedules so we're not doing too much at one time and not enough at other times. Whenever we feel like giving up under the pressure of responsibilities, we can remember there are always solutions. Nothing is cast in stone, unless we want it to be.

Tonight I can begin thinking about making changes in my responsibilities. I can ask for help and do some rearranging so no day is overwhelming.

You have no idea what a poor opinion I have of myself, and how little I deserve it.
— William Gilbert

Can we say "I like me" and really mean it? To say that statement and mean it we have to like everything about ourselves: our good qualities as well as our bad, our appearance, the way we interact with others, the way we express ourselves. We don't have to love everything about us, but we need to learn to like ourselves.

Liking ourselves doesn't mean we approve of certain traits or behaviors. But we can accept them. We don't deserve the low opinion we may have of ourselves. We aren't so bad. We make mistakes as well as everyone else. We aren't the most perfect companion, lover, friend, or parent. Neither is anyone else.

There are very likable people inside us that struggle to change and become better. We deserve to like ourselves for who we are and who we're becoming.

Tonight I will think of at least five qualities about myself I like. I can say "I like me" and mean it.

The sculptor produces the beautiful statue by chipping away such parts of the marble block as are not needed—it is a process of elimination.
—Elbert Hubbard

When people set aside items for a yard sale, they tag things no longer needed. When we look at things we might sell, we might be surprised to remember how badly we felt we needed or wanted a particular item. But over time, or because we grew up, we found we could eliminate the once-treasured item from our lives.

We'll find we can do the same process of elimination with our character defects. Some may be impossible to eliminate now for whatever reason. Yet over time, we may find ourselves outgrowing this defect or gathering courage to eliminate it.

Tonight we're on our way to sculpting beautiful people—ourselves. We may have a long way to go in forming our shapes, but we're in no hurry. Every so often we'll eliminate a piece of marble so more of our beautiful shapes are revealed. Before long, we'll have smooth, striking statues for all to behold.

I'm on my way to sculpting a beautiful me. Every day I will sculpt some more and eliminate things I don't need.

The error of the past is the success of the future. A mistake is evidence that someone tried to do something.

—*Anonymous*

Remember our high school science fairs? There was always one entry that seemed to be everything the judges wanted: it was perfect, innovative, instructive. Yet there were other entries that would also win awards, and we may have wondered why they won. They seemed to be simplistic and maybe messy. So why did they win recognition?

Most often it was because of the effort someone put into the entry. Not every winner has to be the most perfect, most innovative, and most instructive. Some are winners because the person who did them made his or her best effort.

The important thing to know tonight is that it's the effort that counts. We don't have to have all the answers, or act in the most mature way, or be the best friend ever. There is room for error in everything because nothing is gained in perfection the first time around. We can make mistakes because mistakes are sometimes the only way to reach perfection, and to measure how hard we've tried.

Have I made mistakes today? Tonight I can see my mistakes as valuable evidence of my efforts.

Give us to go blithely on our business this day,
bring us to our resting beds weary and content
and undishonored, and grant us in the end the
gift of sleep.

—Robert Louis Stevenson

Tonight, our reward for the day is sleep. To make sleep peaceful and relaxing, and filled with pleasant thoughts, we can spend time gently closing our minds to the day's events.

We can walk down a pleasant, nature-filled path in our minds. With each step we can move farther away from the day's activities and the many tasks we did or left undone. Look around us. We can see lakes and mountains and hear the soothing sounds of a speeding stream. Nothing is important now except peace of mind and the hours ahead in which our minds will be at peace.

Before we shut off the light we can spend a few minutes visualizing our pleasant nature walks. We can think *Let Go and Let God* and feel the day's tensions and pressures fall from our shoulders. Today has been good. We can close our eyes now and let the reward of sleep drift over us.

My day has been good. I have done well. I am satisfied and ready to let sleep overtake me.

AUGUST

. . . each cycle of the tide is valid; each cycle of the wave is valid; each cycle of a relationship is valid.

—Anne Morrow Lindbergh

Any photograph will show us a moment frozen in time. Forever after, anyone who views that picture will see that moment as it was.

Many things in our lives have cycles. Nothing ever stays the same from one minute to the next. We may not like change in our relationships, for we may expect that any variation from our happy moments will mean pain or loss or rejection. Even in a relationship's dark moments of anger and pain, we may fear changes that can bring happiness, hope, and success.

Yet change is a valid measurement of growth and time. It has as natural a rhythm as the ebb and flow of the ocean, the change of the seasons, the waxing and waning of the moon, the rise and set of the sun. Tonight, we can be assured that our relationships are right where they need to be in their natural places.

Tonight help me experience the natural rhythms in my relationships without fear.

Worry is a thin stream of fear trickling through the mind. If encouraged, it cuts a channel into which all other thoughts are drained.
—Arthur Somers Roche

A trickle of water that drains down the side of a hill poses no problem to the hill, its vegetation, or the people living in the valley. But if that trickle grows into a stream, the water will erode a path, carrying along plants, rocks, and soil, endangering the lives and property of the people in the valley.

When a worry nags us, it is like that trickle. It poses little threat to us and can be stopped at any time because it is so small. But if we let more worrisome thoughts feed into the stream, we will allow it to grow until all of our thoughts and energy are focused on one worry that has attained great power.

We all have things we worry about. But we don't have to give these worries more than passing acknowledgment. The trickles that run through our minds are okay to have. But to keep them at that size, we need to remember what is important to us at this very moment. We don't need to let the worries grow.

I have worries just like everyone else. However, I don't have to dwell upon my worries or make them any bigger than what they are.

What must I do is all that concerns me—not what people think. It is easy in the world to live after the world's opinion; it is easy in solitude to live after our own—but the great man is he who in the midst of the crowd keeps with perfect sweetness the independence of solitude.
—Ralph Waldo Emerson

Many times we are like chameleons, changing colors to please others. We may hide our true feelings and pretend to be happy and content, not wanting to hurt someone close.

Chameleons survive because they are adept at hiding from predators. We may feel we are living well when we hide our true feelings. Yet who is seeing the real side of us? Aren't we ignoring our needs and making someone else's more important?

Today we may have changed colors to please others. But we don't have to be chameleons. There are no predators out there—only people, just like us. Their thoughts and feelings may be different from ours, but that's okay. We all have our own brilliant colors to show.

I have beautiful colors to show off. Tonight, I'll remind myself that I do not need to hide.

*The height of wisdom is to take things as they are
. . . to endure what we cannot evade.*
—Montaigne

What are some of the things we dread? As children
we probably dreaded school and occasions when we
had to dress up. As students we most likely dreaded
tests. As adults we may now dread job performance
reviews or visits with our parents. We may have other
dreads such as going to a dentist or doctor, purchasing
a major appliance, or making changes.

Wisdom is the ability to acknowledge the dread and
not run from it. It's okay to feel dread: wanting to
postpone, feeling sick, having an anxiety attack, becoming dependent on another to help us out. As long
as we don't succumb to those feelings—as powerful as
they may be—we will endure the dreaded event.

Nothing lasts forever. Job reviews and dentist visits
comprise only a portion of a day. If we can accept
these dreaded events as inconveniences, we will have
a more mature approach to them instead of magnify-
ing them. The steps to overcoming dread are simple:
accept, let go, and do it!

*Are there events I dread tonight? I can remember the three
steps to overcoming dread and work through my feelings.*

I still find each day too short for all the thoughts I want to think, all the walks I want to take, all the books I want to read, and all the friends I want to see.

—John Burroughs

We may look upon richness as an abundance of wealth. Some of us may believe if we only made more money our problems would be solved. Yet we've also heard the phrase, "Money doesn't buy everything." And, because we know that's true, we may question just how we get the riches in our lives.

If we put aside all the insignificant things, we may find we have more time and attention to pay to important people and things. By focusing on the things most important to us, we would find ourselves with more time to do what we want.

Worrying over minor details, fretting over some misplaced item, or whining about some unobtainable desire only serves to distract us. We can increase the richness in our lives by eliminating whatever robs us of our peace of mind.

Tonight I can choose between wealth and poverty. What can I give up in order to enrich my life?

*I offer you no reward for being loyal to me, and
surely I do not threaten you with pain, penalty,
and dire disaster if you are indifferent to me.*
—Elbert Hubbard

We can learn a great deal about unselfish love from
a pet. A cat or dog stays with us despite mixed messages of "Come here, I need you," and "Go away,
you're bothering me." They're always there for us and
expect nothing in return.

Are we as loyal to our friends, or do we demand
they be there for us when we need them? If they don't
show up, or they let us down, or they give disapproval, do we write them off? Being a friend or having
one doesn't mean making demands. It also doesn't
mean seeking retaliation if our demands aren't met.

We can allow others to show us friendship without
making demands upon them. This means accepting
their attention and love, as well as their lack of attention and their silence. Friends are not promises to be
kept or admirers to be courted. Friends are blessings.
The more we treat them like blessings, the more
friends we'll be blessed with.

*How well did I treat my friends today? I can let my friends
be themselves, showing their own forms of love and
respect.*

I been so busy thinking about Him I never truly notice nothing God make. Not a blade of corn (how it do that?) not the color purple (where it come from?). Not the little wildflowers. Nothing.
—Alice Walker,
The Color Purple

Each snowflake that falls from the sky has a different pattern. Every fall foliage season is a spectacular pallet of oranges, reds, and yellows. The height of the giant redwoods is astounding. The rainbow after a rainstorm, the camouflage of nature's insects and animals, and the majesty of the mountains are just a few of the natural wonders of the world.

How often do we notice these wonders? How often do we go out of our way to discover a new path, or vary our schedules to include a new hobby, task, or person in our lives?

Tonight we can slow down the pace and notice the things around us. If we can quietly think about these things for a few minutes, then we have meditated upon them and brought ourselves spiritually closer to them. We can begin to notice the creations of our Higher Power and appreciate their beauty.

Am I grateful for the creations of my Higher Power?

The man who goes alone can start today, but he who travels with another must wait till that other is ready.

—Henry David Thoreau

Do we ever change our minds or our plans, depending on what another person says? Maybe we'd like some time alone, but because another wants us to do something else we bow to those wishes. We may even feel lost unless someone provides us with suggestions of things to do.

It's up to us to undertake our own journeys in life. If we're always waiting to see what someone else will do, we'll be waiting forever. We need to make independent choices and decisions without feeling linked to the wishes or desires of others.

Tonight we can begin our journeys by making our choices. Our desires are important, and it's equally important to stick to them no matter what the wishes of another.

It's okay to change my mind and my plans if I wish, choose to be alone, or ask to be with another. The decision is mine to make.

I have accepted fear as a part of life—specifically the fear of change ... I have gone ahead despite the pounding in the heart that says: turn back. ...

—Erica Jong

There comes a time in every horror movie when we know something bad is going to happen. We can feel the tension and the pounding of our hearts, and we may want to scream at the actors to alert them of danger. But that's only a movie.

We will feel fear whenever we see darkness and not light. We will feel fear whenever we imagine someone or something is out to get us. Before the program, our lives were filled with many real dangers, yet we may not have seen them as real. Today our lives can be filled with safety, security, and harmony, if we see and face real dangers and not imaginary ones.

Life isn't a horror movie where danger is always lurking around the corner. There isn't some big monster out to grab us. The only fears we have tonight are those that spring forth from the shadows of the unknown.

Tonight I can remember my fears are based on making changes in myself for the better. It's okay to be afraid, as long as I don't let this fear rule—and ruin—my life.

. . . We look upon Niagara and say, wonderful thinking nothing of all that makes its glory and majesty possible. We look upon a man or woman of character; we are lost in admiration, but we omit to consider the thousand influences, conscious and unconscious, which have gone to make up the result.

—Stephen S. Wise

We are molded and influenced by countless people, beginning with our parents. Relatives, friends, lovers, co-workers, and neighbors all play a role in making us who we are.

We may wish to blame others for who we are when we see only our negative sides. But we have positive sides, too, that may be admired. And just like our negative sides, people help shape our positive sides.

A lake at the base of a mountain range gets its origin from the highest mountain, when its snowy cap is melted by the sun. This one trickle of melted snow expands into a stream, and then a river, by the countless trickles that feed into it. We, too, are like that lake. We are beautiful as we stand alone. Yet we must remember all the energy that contributed to our beauty.

———————————

Tonight I can be grateful for the people who have had a positive influence on me. I am beautiful because they showed me I am.

Listen, or thy tongues will keep thee deaf.
                    —Native American proverb

The Tower of Babel was so named because all the
people who were working on it were speaking different languages all at the same time. Construction didn't
succeed because no one listened to one another. With
all the babbling, it was as if they were deaf.

Most of us have the ability to hear. Yet we don't
make full use of it when we choose to talk constantly,
bending someone else's ear as we endlessly babble on.
We don't use our ability to listen at meetings or to
family members or our lover as well as we could. We
can become so wrapped up in listening to ourselves
that we can't hear anyone else.

It's our choice to remain deaf to other voices but
our own. This self-imposed deafness can deprive us of
valuable experience and knowledge from those working on the same issues as we are. To improve our hearing, we need to shut our mouths and open our ears.
To hear other voices can be music to our ears!

*I can stop being deaf to other voices around me. There is a
symphony of strength and serenity if I only stop to hear it!*

The biggest lesson I've learned ... was that if you have all the fresh water you want to drink and all the food you want to eat, you ought never to complain about anything.

—Eddie Rickenbacker

For almost twenty-one days, Eddie Rickenbacker floated aimlessly in a life raft in the Pacific Ocean. That experience helped him see life differently than most people, because he learned to focus on the basics of happiness and contentment—food and water.

Are we satisfied with what we have, or do we believe happiness is achieved after we have a new appliance, a new car, a different house, more money, a better partner, or two more years of recovery? Are we always looking to the next thing we need before we'll be satisfied, rather than appreciating the basics around us?

Keep it Simple reminds us that we need very little to survive comfortably. Food to eat, a place to live, a way to make money, and a belief in a Higher Power are some of the things our early settlers gave great thanks for. Have we given thanks today for simple things that help us stay happy, healthy, and hopeful?

Tonight, I can give thanks for the many simple blessings around me.

Nobody grows old merely by a number of years. We grow old by deserting our ideals. Years may wrinkle the skin, but to give up enthusiasm wrinkles the soul.

—*Samuel Ullman*

Today we see more young people in the program. We may look at them and think, "If only I had found the program at their age. I would have so much more time to live and grow."

We've heard it said, "You are as young as you feel." Although physically we may feel not so young, that phrase refers to our state of mind and the belief in our hearts. To feel younger, imagine the program has given us new life, and we can measure our age in terms of our time since recovery.

Perhaps today we are one year old or five or more. In the program we are all children, not adults. We are all learning for the first time how to walk on our own, how to speak our minds, and how to take care of ourselves. We are not old . . . we are but babes ready to learn and grow!

Tonight I can forget my chronological age and think instead of my youth in the program. I am young, with lots of time to grow.

I am sick and tired of the snivelers, the defeated, and the whiners. I am sick and tired of being expected to believe that ugliness is beauty, that melancholy is man's sole pleasure, that delinquency is delight, that laughter is something to be ashamed of.

—John Mason Brown

Every year businesses go through their files, throwing out old information and papers, and reorganizing remaining files. We can do some cleaning of the message files we keep in our heads.

Stored inside us are messages that no longer hold true: "You're a bad person." "You shouldn't show your feelings." "If you cry, you're not a man." "You'll never amount to anything." "Nobody loves you." We can toss out these old messages. We have learned things are not the way those messages claim they are.

We can start new message files: "I'm a nice person." "Crying is a good way to express my feelings." "It's important for me to show how I feel." "I'm doing wonderful things for myself." "People love me." There's no need to hold on to old files when we have wonderful new ones.

I can start weeding out negative messages in my mind. What are some new messages I can put there instead?

Laughing ... stirs up the blood, expands the chest, electrifies the nerves, clears away the cobwebs from the brain, and gives the whole system a cleansing rehabilitation.

—Anonymous

One of the greatest gifts the program gives us is the ability to laugh. Laughter is one of the best forms of relaxation. But unless we allow ourselves to see the humorous things in life, we'll have a difficult time bringing out this delightful release.

One way to begin is to practice laughing when we're alone. A loud "ha, ha, ha" while we're driving can startle us at first. But with a little practice we will see the humor in our laugh sessions and laugh without a cue.

There are a lot of things to laugh about in life. But laughter isn't always easy to find. We may have to go out of our way to look for the humor in some situations. We don't have to be comedians to be able to laugh. All we have to do is want to see the other side of life—the humorous side.

Tonight I can try to see things in a humorous light instead of with a heavy, depressing view. There are things that will make me laugh if I try to find them.

If a ship has been sunk, I can't bring it up. If it is going to be sunk, I can't stop it. I can use my time much better working on tomorrow's problem than by fretting about yesterday's.
—Admiral Ernest J. King

Have we ever really thought about the things we cannot change? We may know we can't change things, but we need to personalize that list. What people can't we change? What places? What things?

Until we make a list, we may spin our wheels trying to change the actions or thoughts of others. We may try to control the lives of our children, relatives, or friends. We may attempt to force attitude changes in the boss, teachers, or co-workers. We may even go so far as to believe we can change traffic patterns, the weather, or the past!

Saying we cannot change things is not enough. We need to recognize what people, places, and things we have been trying to change. By listing them, we will recognize there is only one thing in our lives that we can change—ourselves.

Who are the people and what are the things I cannot change? After I list these things, I can begin working on who I can change—myself.

. . . there are hundreds of tasks we feel we must accomplish in the day, but if we do not take them one at a time and let them pass through the day slowly and evenly, as do the grains of sand passing through the narrow neck of the hourglass, then we are bound to break our own physical or mental structure.

—Ted Bengermino

Our mental and physical states at bedtime are important. If we are tense, edgy, and feel a sense of failure and defeat, our sleep will probably be restless and unpeaceful. But if we go to sleep tonight feeling we have put the day to rest in peace and acceptance, our sleep will likely be restorative and refreshing.

What difference does it make if things are left undone tonight? Will it matter ten years from now? Nothing is so important that we should carry tension and worry into our relaxation time. What is important is our ability to accept the day's events by the time we're ready to sleep. The most important thing right now is to get the rest we need to be in good shape for tomorrow. The day is done, and so is the day's work.

I am ready to relax in a peaceful, restful sleep. I can loosen the day's tension from my shoulders and meditate on acceptance.

For every ailment under the sun,
There is a remedy, or there is none;
If there be one, try to find it;
If there is none, never mind it.
　　　　　　　　　　　—Mother Goose

Long ago peddlers sold instant remedies for everything from illness to baldness. "Miracle" cures did a brisk business because people always wanted to try the next instant solution to persistent ailments and problems.

Are we still looking for a miracle cure, one that will make us that person we always wanted to be? Although those peddlers sold a lot of cures, none beat the time-tested methods of assured success for curing worry and woes: plenty of time, a good deal of effort, and an acceptance of things that can't be changed.

There are miracle cures in the program, but they are not instant. In fact, sometimes we can't even feel the restorative powers until months later. But if we continue to take them, the cures we get in the program are guaranteed for life. Our lives can be free from worries and woes with the program.

Tonight I can plan to get a good, healthy dose of the cure by attending a meeting tomorrow, reading literature, or talking with my sponsor.

When we hate our enemies, we give them power over us—power over our sleep, our appetites, and our unhappiness. Our hate is not hurting them at all, but it is turning our days and nights into hellish turmoil.

—*Dale Carnegie*

Hate is such a strong feeling, and it may be part of our black-and-white way of looking at things: right or wrong, yes or no, now or never, love or hate.

Spending our precious nights nurturing a strong dislike for a co-worker, boss, teacher, parent, former lover, or even a stranger is a waste of time and energy. It becomes an obsession, and we know how easy it is for us to find an obsession and hold on to it dearly.

Instead of making one person our focus, we can think of all the people who are near and dear to us. We can visualize the faces of those who give us strength and hope and comfort and let their images stay in our minds and hearts.

Instead of seeing one face in the crowd, I will see many.

You can observe a lot just by watchin'.
　　　　　　　　　　　　　—Yogi Berra

Our sight is one of our most valuable senses. We can lose our hearing and have our senses of smell, taste, and touch eliminated, yet our eyes will provide us with all the information we need for hearing, smelling, tasting, and feeling.

We can picture in our minds a person we admire greatly. We can even visualize that person's expressions. We may be able to see that person's confidence, strength, and unity just in those expressions. We can imagine the person's lips moving and, without hearing a voice, we can see by the body movements how the person presents a being full of confidence and hope.

Can we picture ourselves and how we come across to others just by what they see? Are our words trying to mask the sad expression on our faces? Are we honest with how we feel and show this? We can let people observe us and let them see openness and honesty through all their senses.

Can the words I speak reflect who I am? Let me observe others and myself to truly feel the real person within.

Fear less, hope more, eat less, chew more, whine less, breathe more, talk less, say more, love more, and all good things will be yours.
—Swedish proverb

What do we have to do to get better in the program? Our first response may be to list all the healthy things we need to do: detach, meditate, pray, share, make phone calls, go to meetings, do the Steps, use the slogans, change behaviors. We soon have constructed an incredible list of dos and don'ts.

But we can *Keep It Simple*. All we need to do is live *One Day at a Time* in a different way than before. There are many positive things we can do, but we don't need to do them all at once.

Tonight we can just be ourselves. We don't need to make drastic changes or have dramatic mood swings or create radical resolutions. All that is asked of us is just to *Keep It Simple*.

Tonight I don't need to make radical changes. Help me Keep It Simple in all the changes I want to make.

Never measure the height of a mountain until you have reached the top. Then you'll see how low it is.

—Dag Hammarskjöld

What happens when we try to pick up a shell or pretty rock that's under water? We may have a difficult time with the play of sunlight and the rippling of water. Because we're outside the water looking in, once our hands enter the water our perspective changes.

Many times the overreacting side of our personalities may blow things out of proportion. Mountains become molehills, and vice versa. Because of our sensitivities, we may find it difficult to be objective during certain situations. Because we're taking risks and feeling more vulnerable, we may blindly build unneeded defenses.

We can try to keep our perspectives in line by pausing before reacting. We can ask ourselves to identify what's happening and what action we need to take, if any. Instead of feeling threatened, subjective, or sensitive, we can use the extra time to get the proper perspective on a situation.

Have I blown anything out of proportion today? I can review the situation in order to get the proper perspective.

You want me to succeed so much.
Could you understand if I failed? . . .
Could you love me if I failed?
—Sister Mary Paul

What is it we fear the most about success? Sometimes we fear we'll fail. But failure isn't as scary as losing the admiration, respect, or even the love of those we're trying to impress.

We sometimes look outside of ourselves too much for the love, rewards, and approval for our actions. We may feel we're not good enough, so we set nearly impossible feats in which we strive to succeed.

Tonight, we're a success. No matter what we've done or what we'll do, we are a success. If we've set out to do something today and fallen short of our goals, we haven't lost the admiration, respect, or love of those around us. There are those who will love us whether we fail or succeed, for they are the ones who love us for ourselves and believe in us. Their love will always be there.

Who loves me and believes in me? Tonight I can be grateful for their love and belief and know that is the greatest success I can achieve.

The message is, "It's okay if you mess up. You should give yourself a break."

—*Billy Joel*

The song "You're Only Human" was written to help teens eliminate suicide as an option to life's problems. It tells them it's okay to make mistakes. In fact, because we're human, we're supposed to make mistakes.

Mistakes don't last forever. They are small events in the larger master plan of life. While a mistake may hurt another or affect the outcome of a situation, a mistake is not so earth-shattering and catastrophic that we can't learn something from it, forgive ourselves, and let it go.

There's no reason to feel we need to punish ourselves if we do something wrong. It's the mature person who can look at a mistake and shrug it off easily. It's the perfectionistic, people-pleasing person that demands retribution for mistakes and never wants to forget them. Which is easier for us to be?

Tonight I can look at my mistakes and know they are signs of my humanness. It is healthy to make a mistake every once in a while and be able to accept it as a normal part of living.

To get peace, if you want it, make for yourselves nests of pleasant thoughts.
—*John Ruskin*

A bird builds its nest by first searching for the perfect twigs, string, and papers. Then it patiently interweaves these materials until its nest achieves the right shape, size, depth, and warmth. Once completed, the bird ceases its work and spends its time nestled comfortably in its home.

To be at peace with ourselves, we have to construct our own nest. This nest doesn't always have to be a place. It can also be found in freedom from negative thinking. Or it can be a time we set aside solely for our enjoyment and relaxation.

Without this time or space, peace will be difficult to achieve. We may see evidence of this in our schedules that allow plenty of time to do but not enough time to just be. Tonight we can start to set aside moments, rearrange schedules, and give ourselves the chance to make our own nest of pleasant thoughts.

Tonight I can find pleasure in today and relax. What pleasant thoughts can I use to build my nest?

The real voyage of discovery consists not in seeking new landscapes but in having new eyes.
—Marcel Proust

How have we felt when we return to our hometowns, childhood homes, old playgrounds, or high schools after years of absence? Suddenly each place isn't as it once seemed because we're looking through the eyes of someone older and changed. Where we once saw our high school through the eyes of students, we now look at it through the eyes of adults—in a much different way.

So it is with all areas of our lives: our jobs, homes, families, friends, or partners. Many of these people and places haven't changed for a long time. Yet, we change every day. Instead of seeing our job as the same old job or our home as the same old home, we can start to look at them differently.

Tonight we don't need to change things on the outside to feel better on the inside. We can change how we look at things from the inside out. We can start to see who and what are outside of us as if we were looking at them for the first time. Tonight the ho-hums in our lives can turn into ah-has just by changing the way we see them.

There may be many things in my life that haven't changed, but I'm not one of them. Tonight I can see them all with new eyes.

How poor are they who have not patience. What wound did ever heal but by degrees?
—William Shakespeare

The broken leg, stitched cut, burned arm, sprained ankle—even the broken heart—all need time to heal. Such healing is a process of slow steps. Each day finds the leg, cut, arm, ankle, or heart a little bit stronger—a little more capable of functioning at full capacity.

The injured football player who paces the sidelines during the championship game can do nothing for his team. He must be patient and know the healing process will allow him to resume his position next season. Those who wish to speed up the healing process are trapped by powerlessness and loss of control.

Patience is more than a virtue. It's the ultimate test in powerlessness. Patience means waiting for people, places, or things beyond our control. Patience means letting go and trusting that a Higher Power is in control. Without patience, we're like the injured athlete filled with pain, misery, and stress. With patience, we become full of acceptance of our current condition and trust it will change.

Do I have patience? Tonight I need to practice patience by letting go and trusting my Higher Power is in control.

*It takes more than a soft pillow to insure sound
sleep.*

—*Anonymous*

Our minds may be the most difficult part of our
bodies to relax. From our toes to our fingertips, we
may find we can easily make the limb and torso muscles grow heavy with relaxation. But when it comes to
the muscle that exists above our necks, we may find
our heads so loaded with facts and feelings that signals
to relax get blocked.

If we were to open the top of our heads and see the
crammed things as slips of paper, what would we
find? On one slip of paper we might see the word
guilt. On another, shame. Others might read anger,
stress, jealousy, pressure, fear, or distrust.

All these papers do is clog the channels of creativity,
fun, and relaxation. When these channels are clogged,
even the most comfortable bed and the softest pillow
won't help us have a peaceful sleep. To make the most
of our relaxation time tonight, we need to place those
papers where they belong—in the trash.

---

*Tonight I can do a little "head cleaning" before I go to
sleep. Help me remove all the unwanted messages and let
the peaceful channels flow free.*

The awareness of the ambiguity of one's highest achievements (as well as one's deepest failures) is a definite symptom of maturity.
—Paul Tillich

While we were still living with the effects of the disease, we may have ridden the roller coaster of highs and lows. But once we got off that crazy ride, we learned life isn't so dramatic. Life has its wonderful moments and its not-so-wonderful ones, but on the whole it takes us on a steady ride.

Once we begin to mature in the program, we learn how to become a passenger of life without gripping the rails and strapping ourselves in. Now we can open our eyes for the whole ride, look around us with wonder and appreciation, and feel less breathless about the movement of it all. Life without the highs and lows is a wonderful trip.

Tonight I can feel the quiet pace of my life and not question whether it is normal. I can relax and trust this quiet pace as a sign of my maturity.

A bit of fragrance always clings to the hand that gives you roses.

—*Chinese proverb*

Remember reading fairy tales where elves would come in the middle of the night to build toys or repair broken dreams or help another have more free time? They would work furiously, yet happily, knowing they were doing something that person really needed or wanted. They asked for no reward; in fact, they didn't even stay long enough to see the surprised, smiling faces. They knew without seeing the results that they were creating happiness and gratefulness in another.

We can do the same thing for others. We can decide to be more caring, to watch for opportunities to reach out to others. We can bring some flowers to a friend. We can remember someone's special treat. We can write a letter or send a card or make a long-distance phone call.

I will brighten the life of another tomorrow, by doing something special and unexpected. I will feel the joy of giving and brighten my day, too!

The secret of being miserable is to have the leisure to bother about whether you are happy or not.

—George Bernard Shaw

How much time do we spend thinking about our problems, our pasts, our miseries? We may spend a great deal of time feeling negative feelings. We may even find ourselves thinking miserably in happy, fun situations.

How much time we spend alone may have a direct bearing on time spent thinking miserable thoughts and feeling miserable about our lives and ourselves. Until we can spend time alone with positive feelings, we may need to depend a great deal on others to spend time with us. We need to change our belief that we will never be happy. To do that, we need to learn from others that things do get better. Tonight, it is up to us to spend our time with good thoughts of including others in our lives. This is the antidote to misery.

Tonight I can choose to be miserable or happy. I can plan some positive actions to avoid misery by including friends and the program in my life.

SEPTEMBER

I like trees because they seem more resigned to
the way they have to live than other things do.
—Willa Cather

If a tree's soil becomes dry or low in valuable minerals, it can't pull up its roots and move to a better place. Instead, the tree spreads its roots deeper and wider, seeking fertile ground. It makes the surrounding soil richer by dropping dead branches and leaves to mulch the ground below. It remains firm in the wind, bends but doesn't break under the weight of ice and snow, and gives shade, shelter, and nourishment to the ground below.

Beginning tonight, if we think of ourselves as trees firmly placed, we can learn to be more accepting of our surroundings. We can learn to grow no matter how difficult it may seem. Such growth can enrich our lives and make us stronger so we don't break with the weight of problems or difficulties. We, too, can be as strong and enduring as trees.

I can learn to move with the winds of change and bend
with the weight of difficulties—and still stand tall and
firm.

And this is my way o' looking at it: there's the sperrit o' God in all things and all times— weekday as well as Sunday—and i' the great works and inventions, and i' the figuring and the mechanics. And God helps us with our headpieces and our hands as well as with our souls. . . .

—George Eliot

The concept of a Higher Power may have been difficult for us to understand as children. But many of us still question the existence of anything beyond us that will help us get well.

A Higher Power's existence can be evidenced in many nonreligious ways. The creative gifts given to an artist, people who smile at us and call us friends— these are evidence of a Higher Power.

The Higher Power of the program is an overriding feeling of peace and serenity. We can take in that feeling when we detach, when we say the Serenity Prayer, when we ask for help, even when we breathe deeply and relax. There is a greater Power for all of us who want to believe, whenever we're ready.

I believe I can find peace and serenity in my life. Tonight I can ask for help to find it.

*Avoid friends and followers who are detrimental
to thy peace of mind and spiritual growth.*
— Tibetan Rosary of Precious Gems

Who are the friends we love tonight? Are they healthy in mind, body, and spirit? Do we learn from them and grow with them? Are they an important part of our lives?

Through our growth in the program, we may look at our friends of the past and recognize they were not the best influences on us. In fact, they may have been as needy, sick, confused, obsessive, and miserable as we were. Perhaps that's why they were our friends: they were just like us. But now we may have different friends and they may be like us: healthier, happier, more mature, and more capable.

The people we choose as our friends validate us and our growth. If we choose to be around unhealthy people, then we, too, are unhealthy. Yet if we choose to be around people concerned about their growth, who ask for help when necessary, who can receive yet also give, then we are like those people. They are the mirrors through which we see ourselves.

When I look in the mirror, what do I see? How can I improve my image and my personal growth?

Loneliness is a bitter thing . . . more bitter when
you think you have been freed from it and find it
returning again.

—Anne Cameron

It is a rare person indeed who never feels lonely. Even when we are surrounded by co-workers, friends, or family, we can still feel lonely. Now that we have the program and our Higher Power, why shouldn't we have feelings of loneliness? "What's wrong with me?" we may cry, thinking we are doing something to cause these feelings.

But feelings of loneliness can reveal our need to get out more, to be with people. We may be so withdrawn into ourselves that we cannot see or hear others around us. Yet they are there. They have been there all day today, and they will continue to be there for us.

If we listen to ourselves, we will be able to hear our needs crying out for attention. If we pay attention to our lonely feelings, we can open ourselves up to the "cures"—a phone call, a walk with a friend, a meeting, or a few hugs!

Help me listen to my loneliness. I can then open myself up
to others.

Rest is not a matter of doing absolutely nothing.
Rest is repair.
                                    —*Daniel W. Josselyn*

When we are sick, it is evident we need rest because our bodies tell us so. But when we are healthy, it is more difficult to hear those messages. So we may work overtime, stay up later, or spend more time on chores or projects.

But if we learn to listen to our bodies, we will pick up subtle messages that signal a need for rest. Tight muscles, a backache, a slight headache, and tired eyes are some of those messages. When the batteries wear down in a flashlight, the light becomes dimmer until it finally goes out. Before our "bulbs" go out and we fall victim to ill health, we need to remember our inner batteries can't run without rest.

Resting doesn't necessarily mean doing nothing. Rest is slowing our pace, becoming less active, less tense. Going to a meeting can be restful. Reading literature, watching television or a movie, listening to music, or talking to friends are all forms of rest. Resting recharges our batteries so we can continue to shine bright and strong.

Tonight I will recharge my batteries so I can shine tomorrow.

Life is an experience of ripening. The green fruit has but small resemblance to that which is matured.

—Charles B. Newcomb

When a lion cub is born, it bears little resemblance to its adult form. As it matures, it still is a far cry from being king of the jungle. It has tiny teeth, small paws, and a clumsy sense of balance. With training and time for growth, it learns to stalk and kill. Finally, it becomes a full-grown, mature lion with thick mane, long teeth, and powerful claws.

Sometimes we are like that cub. We are acquiring skills, learning to grow emotionally, spiritually, and physically. Our footing may be clumsy, our efforts not always successful. But there are others who are experienced and can show us the way.

There is a lion inside of each of us: strong, sure, and proud. We are growing and maturing toward this final form. Every day our footing becomes a little surer, our confidence greater, and our beliefs in our abilities stronger. Life is a process of growing from cub to lion, and each day takes us closer.

Tonight I can feel the growth within me. I have strength, sureness, and pride that are just beginning to bud.

We have loved the stars too fondly to be fearful of the night.
—Inscription in crypt of Allegheny Observatory, University of Pittsburgh

Some people so love their work or hobbies that they almost seem to become different people when they're involved with what they love to do. Their voices becomes animated, their eyes light up, and they feel energized all over. What do we have in our lives that makes us feel that way?

If we don't love doing something—just one thing—then we are missing out on an experience that drives us and challenges us to learn and grow.

Loving what we do teaches us much about our abilities. Through the program of recovery, we may be learning we have a great deal of skill and talent we never knew we had. Developing these skills and talents can yield us more pleasure than we've ever had.

What do I love to do? Tonight I can find pleasure in recognizing my skills and talents.

Don't try to saw sawdust.

—Dale Carnegie

The pile of sawdust that gathers under our wood-working can never go back to its previous form. The lumber used to build a house can never return to the forest as a tree. That is a law of nature: whatever takes on a new form can never return to its original state. We may believe this statement as a law of nature, but may not believe it also applies to the past.

We can never go back to the past; the past can never become the present. We are not the same people today that we were when we were five years old, ten years old, or twenty years old. If we are always trying to live in the past, then we are trying to saw sawdust. To live in the present, we must work with new pieces of wood and make new piles of sawdust.

Tonight I can stop living in the past and see the present for what it really is: clean, fresh, and new.

*It would all be so beautiful if people were just
kind . . . what is more wise than to be kind? And
what is more kind than to understand?*
—*Thomas Tryon*

Sometimes we may think life is pretty unkind. Such
a feeling could have started years ago when we were
brought up in an alcoholic home. That feeling might
have continued as we agonized through our addictions. Now we may even be able to make mental lists
of those unkind things in our lives: family, loved ones,
bosses, major disappointments, disease. "Life has
dealt me a terrible blow!" we may moan.

But kindness can start with us! How many times today could we have smiled instead of frowned?
Couldn't we have let someone ahead of us in traffic
instead of barreling on by? Perhaps we could have
picked up the telephone and spoken a few kind words
to a friend or family member.

We can't change the unkindness of today. But we
can make changes in how we behave tomorrow.

---

*Is there someone who needs my kindness and
understanding? How can I show this kindness?*

*Nowadays some people expect the door of
opportunity to be opened with an electric eye.*
—*Anonymous*

"Great Expectations" may be an appropriate title for
certain scenes in our lives. If we act a certain way, do
certain things, or think in a certain way, we may believe these actions will have an expected reaction. But
we'll have a rude awakening when we find this isn't
necessarily so.

It's as if we stepped on the automatic doormat to a
grocery store when the mat wasn't operating. We'll
crash into the door if we expect it to open every time.
Similarly, we can't have expectations about the people
in our lives or we'll crash into defeat, hurt, and
rejection.

It's okay to behave toward others in a loving and
kind manner. In return, others may become more
kind and loving toward us. This treatment won't come
to us because of our expectations, but because others
decide to treat us in this way. If we change our expectations, we may receive many pleasant surprises.

*Do I expect people to treat me in a way they don't want
to? Tonight I can let go of my expectations. What's most
important is my behavior.*

Our belief at the beginning of a doubtful undertaking is the one thing that insures the successful outcome of our venture.
—William James

How often have we heard ourselves say, "Well, I'll try, but I probably won't do it right." We're setting ourselves up for defeat, right from the start. With that much negative energy, certainly our ventures will turn out just the way we predicted. If pessimists had always been right, we would be living differently. We might still believe the world is flat, because Columbus wouldn't have taken his voyage. We might still be reading by candlelight, because Edison wouldn't have invented the light bulb. It would take us days to cross the country, because the Wright brothers would have believed only birds can fly.

Some things we do will succeed, and some will fail. But in order to make successes happen, we need to believe they can occur. And we also need to believe in ourselves, believe that we can make things happen. Since we've lived for so long without faith in ourselves, what will it hurt to give it a try?

Higher Power, help me fill my mind tonight with thoughts of success and a belief in myself.

Love does not consist of gazing at each other but in looking together in the same direction.
—Antoine de Saint-Exupery

When we're addicted to a person all we can see is that person. Time moves slowly when we're apart, but passes quickly when we're together. We may feel panicky during even the most minor of separations and believe that we are fused into one being.

Loving relationships are not made by taking prisoners. Love is neither hypnotism nor possessiveness. Love is simply a sharing between two people. Many times this sharing involves movement in the same direction toward a mutual goal. Even though we're sharing the same path, we're not sharing the same body and mind.

A successful relationship is one in which we feel it would be okay even if we weren't with the other person. To be able to stand alone as firmly as when we're with another means we've found some sense of self-esteem and self-respect. We can love another and, at the same time, love ourselves.

Is my loving relationship healthy? Tonight I can work on my self-esteem and self-respect and trust I am a good person with or without a partner.

The cure for grief is motion.
—*Elbert Hubbard*

Anniversaries of death, separation, and loss are difficult times. We can be feeling fine one month and then suddenly feel tremendous sadness, pain, and anger during the next. A quick look at our calendars may reveal a reason for our feelings, for we may have experienced something particularly trying at that time.

It's okay to relive an event and our feelings about it, as long as we don't wallow in the past or try to use the event as a reason for all our present difficulties. Grieving is a process that can proceed only when we are in motion.

How do we get in motion? We can imagine we're sitting in a small room of horrible-smelling cigar smoke. We can sit there and feel uncomfortable or even nauseous, or we can leave the room. That's how we get in motion—by simply getting up and moving.

Tonight I can move out of my chair of painful memories. I can think of ways to get in motion and cure these sad feelings. Then I can relax and have a peaceful night's sleep.

Faith is the bird that feels the light when the dawn is still dark.
—*Sir Rabindranath Tagore*

The bird that sings long before the sun has risen is strong evidence of faith. For that bird trusts the sky will soon lighten, the sun will rise, and the world will come alive. It is when the bird won't sing at such a time that we know it has lost faith in the great continuum of things.

Even when things seem darkest for us, we can still sing. Even in our grief or loneliness or fear, we can find a voice within us that will help us have faith that all things change, all wounds heal, all is eased through the passage of time.

We hear people tell us things get better. They do. Of that we can be certain, for it's as sure as the rising sun. There isn't a day that won't have light. There isn't a night that won't have a rising sun at its end. There isn't a problem that won't have a solution, a teardrop that won't have a smile, a weary soul that won't be energized once again. Tonight we can sing, for we can have faith in the rising sun.

Things aren't as bad as they may seem tonight. There is hope, because there is always change.

Whatever course you decide upon, there is always someone to tell you you are wrong. There are always difficulties arising which tempt you to believe that your critics are right. To map out a course of action and follow it to an end requires ... courage.

—Ralph Waldo Emerson

When we first entered the program, someone may have said to us, "Oh, you don't have a problem. You don't need that program." That person may have dismissed our reasons with countless excuses, saying that our decision was silly or foolish, that someday we'd come to our senses.

At first we may have believed our critics. The program certainly wasn't easy. Maybe our circumstances weren't as bad as we thought, compared to others'. Maybe we looked around the meeting room and didn't see people of the same age, the same sex, or the same background. Maybe we felt we didn't belong.

But as we became familiar with the Steps and the principles of the program, we realized we could relate to others and benefit from what they had to say. We, too, belonged.

Tonight, help me be grateful for the courage it took for me to stay in the program.

Let us not look back in anger, nor forward in fear, but around us in awareness.
—James Thurber

What is it we fear the most? Going into a grocery store or going to a gathering of strangers? If we teach ourselves to look not in fear but in awareness, we might see the grocery store's well-stocked delicatessen or the lovely outfit worn by someone at a social gathering.

Who makes us angry? Perhaps the boss does, or maybe a loved one. If we look at him or her not in anger but in awareness, we might see the boss has many tensions and pressures, or a loved one is tired and can't be supportive.

If we look only at our feelings of anger or fear, then those are all we'll see. But if we look around and become aware of the issues of anger or fear, suddenly the anger and fear won't be the focus anymore. Through awareness, we'll learn more about people and we'll gain a greater understanding of their behaviors. Through this awareness, we'll change our reactions of fear and anger to understanding and acceptance.

I can become aware of my feelings and understand them. Then I can work on changing these feelings for the better.

If you make an error, use it as a stepping stone to a new idea you might not otherwise have discovered.

—*Anonymous*

Sometimes we struggle so hard to become perfect human beings that we may view any minor errors of the day as earth-shattering mistakes from which we might never recover. Instead of seeing our errors as entirely human and forgivable, we may sink into feelings of hopelessness and despair.

We can choose to berate ourselves for our errors, or we can see such errors as lessons to learn from. When we were in school, our teachers used tests to measure our capacity for learning. Today, life is our test, and our grades depend upon how well we learn from our errors.

Some of our greatest thinkers used their errors to discover medical cures, time-saving inventions, or scientific theories. The errors of today can become just the stepping stones we need to cross the river of recovery tonight.

Did I make any errors today? How can I learn from them tonight?

Consider the postage stamp: its usefulness consists in the ability to stick to one thing until it gets there.

—*Josh Billings*

We can go to one store and buy an appliance, a shirt, a fishing pole, perfume, shoes, a stereo, and a saber saw. One-stop shopping is convenient, but it has one major drawback. Because of the diversity of products sold, there's no specialization. The sales clerk's knowledge about the saber saw and the shirt will probably be about the same—just enough to sell, but not enough to provide in-depth information.

If we work on several parts of our personalities at once, we'll be like that clerk. To do our best, we need to spend time, brainpower, and perhaps muscle power on just one task. We need to become a specialist in what we're working on for that moment.

If we're hard at work on many changes in our lives, we'll only be setting ourselves up for defeat. The attention we devote to one change deprives another change of the time and effort it needs. To make a change, we need to become a specialist in that change. Then the change we make will be beneficial and lasting.

What is one change I can work on beginning tonight? I will stay focused on that change, giving it my concentrated effort.

When the friendly lights go out, there is a light by which the heart sees.
—Olga Rosmanith

Coming home at night to an unlit house or apartment can be frightening. As we frantically grope for a light switch, we may stumble over tables and chairs that seem to have shifted position in the dark. Yet once the lights go on, we feel an instantaneous burst of relief as we once again view our familiar surroundings.

We do not always need bright lights to find our way in the dark. Faith in a Higher Power that watches over us at all times of our lives is our inner light. This light burns as brightly as our belief. If we are filled with fear, doubt, and insecurity, then we will stumble. But if we are filled with faith, hope, and trust, our feet are always secure.

If we can learn to trust that light within us, we will no longer be frightened of the night. We will not have such a panicked need to flutter from light to light. We will be secure in ourselves, no matter where we are.

Tonight I can remember I am the lighter of my internal lamp.

What [we] usually ask of God . . . is that two
and two not make four.

—*Anonymous*

Wouldn't it be nice if . . . If only . . . What I wish
would happen is . . . Imagine if . . . I should have . . .
Don't these unfinished statements sound familiar?
They usually occur when we're looking away from the
reality of a situation to the fantasy of what might have
been.

We may do the same wishful thinking in our
prayers. Do we still ask for our Higher Power to make
our parents or child or brother or sister or lover or
spouse stop drinking or using drugs? Do we ask for
material things?

Our Higher Power isn't a fairy godmother sent to us
to grant us any wish we'd like. Our Higher Power
deals in realities, not wishful thinking. We, too, need
to deal in realities when we pray. That way, we have a
much better chance of having our prayers answered.

How can I make my prayers more real tonight? I can ask
for things I know are possible instead of impossible.

The great victories of life are oftenest won in a quiet way, and not with alarms and trumpets.
—Benjamin N. Cardozo

How do we know we're getting better? What do we think will happen when we exhibit mature behavior and a positive outlook?

Sometimes we may expect too much from recovery. The successes we have and the achievements we make will not be greeted by fanfare and celebration. Sometimes we won't get any recognition. We might even get disapproval for our mature, positive behaviors.

It's up to us to recognize our victories. We can celebrate such joyous times with a smile or a nod, by making a notation in a journal, or by sharing it at a meeting or in a telephone call. Victory after victory, we will come to realize the most important thing about our achievements is not the recognition but the peaceful, satisfied feeling we have inside.

What were my victories today? Tonight I can celebrate these victories with the wonderful feelings of pride, satisfaction, and good self-esteem.

Live so that you wouldn't be ashamed to sell the family parrot to the town gossip.
—Will Rogers

We may have been brought up to feel a great deal of guilt and shame over the actions of our alcoholic families. As we grew older we may have chosen to act inappropriately toward others so we could continue to feel the guilt and shame that had become so familiar to us.

Are we ashamed or guilty about our behaviors today? Chances are we have so improved our attitudes and our self-image that we now act in mature, responsible ways. We may feel quite proud today about the good people we are becoming.

Today we may feel a lot less fear about our actions. We may be more confident that we aren't antagonizing people anymore or making a spectacle of ourselves. Tonight we can be proud of who we are and project this pride to others.

Tonight I feel I'm on the right path. I'm no longer filled with guilt or shame about my actions. I'm proud of me!

No one can really pull you up very high—you lose your grip on the rope. But on your own two feet you can climb mountains.

—Louis Brandeis

Depending upon people, places, or things to help us live our lives is a sure setup for disappointment and failure. No one person or geographic location or material item can give us answers. None of them can bring us happiness, security, maturity, or faith.

We have been given everything we need to find our own answers. Although today may have been filled with questions, we can remember now that we have the tools we need.

Our Higher Power has brought people to us who we need to hear. Our path has led us onto a well-traveled road with a foundation of strength. By the Grace of God—and our fellow travelers—we can follow this road to the greatest of heights.

How can I use the resources my Higher Power gave me to find my own two feet?

Worry is most apt to ride you ragged not when you are in action, but when the day's work is done. Your imagination can run riot then . . . your mind is like a motor operating without its load.

—James L. Mursell

Each day we may have full-time activities: jobs, school, family, or hobbies. The hours we spend in those activities are usually focused on the tasks at hand. But when they are done and we're left with free time, we may find ourselves cultivating a new interest: worry.

During the day, we are like a train engine. For as long as we stay on the tracks, keeping busy, we move easily. But when the day's activities are done, we are like a derailed engine. The power still makes the wheels spin, but we are going nowhere.

We don't have to be on full speed, going nowhere, as we fill our minds with worry. When the day's work is done on a railroad, the engines are guided onto sidetracks to cool until morning. Tonight we can guide the engines of our minds onto sidetracks of relaxation and rest. We can cool our activities until morning.

I don't need to fill my mind with worry tonight. I can rest and relax my mind by bringing peace to my heart.

We should think seriously before we slam doors, before we burn bridges, before we saw off the limb on which we find ourselves sitting.
—*Richard L. Evans*

Many of us have difficult days. People disappoint us. Events or circumstances upset us. Anger may be our sole feeling at such times. Unfortunately, we may act upon that anger hastily by saying things we later regret, by making shortsighted decisions, or even by slamming a door in someone's face.

Sometimes a slammed door won't open again. Sometimes people we insult or snap at will back off from us. Sometimes decisions we make in anger and haste cannot be changed—or may take considerable time and effort to undo.

Angry moments do not have to erupt into fiery volcanoes. If we learn to sit with our anger awhile until we are calmer and more rational, we can avoid shameful, regretful results. Today's anger does not need to erupt tonight toward any person, place, or thing. Tonight we can let the dust settle and tempers cool while time helps us get things into perspective. We who wait are both wise and mature.

How can I use time to help heal the sores of anger?

I will not meddle with that which I cannot mend.
—*Thomas Fuller*

Sometimes we can effect change. Speaking up about something, suggesting an improvement, or learning a new skill can bring about a longed-for change. But we have to change ourselves first, not anyone, anywhere, or anyplace else.

We can take a moment now to think of those people or things we tried to change today. Then we can resolve not to keep trying to cause change or keep wishing things could change. If a button falls off our shirt, we can pick up a needle and thread and sew it back on. But if we see someone on the street without a button, we can't change that situation. By looking to ourselves and mending our own fences, we won't so likely try to mend the fences of others.

Tonight I can think of people, places, and things I cannot change. Then I can resolve to leave them alone and work on me.

You who are letting miserable misunderstandings
run on from year to year, meaning to clear them
up some day . . . if you could only know and see
and feel all of a sudden that time is short, how it
would break the spell!

—*Phillips Brooks*

The story of the Hatfields and the McCoys is an intense lesson in unforgiveness. Generation after generation honored a long-standing feud. After a while, no
one was quite sure how it all started. What seemed
more important was how to continue it.

Are there people in our lives toward whom we feel
bitterness or hatred? Why? Do we remember why our
gripe with them started? Does it really matter now?
What are the benefits of hanging on to feelings of
unforgiveness?

It takes so much energy to remain cold and aloof to
those people. We can be feeling relaxed and at peace
until they walk into a room. Tonight we can ask ourselves if honoring a long-standing feud is wise or just
willful.

Am I holding on to feelings of anger or bitterness when it
would be wiser to forgive and let go? Tonight I can make a
wise choice for my course of action.

When you have shut the doors and darkened your room, remember never to say that you are alone; for God is within, and your genius is within, and what need have they of light to see what you are doing?

—*Epictetus*

As adults we may feel very secretive about the ways in which we fall asleep. Some of us may have a night-light in our room, fall asleep to music, or tightly hug a stuffed animal. Each of these ways is designed to make us feel safer—less alone in the dark.

None of us is ever alone, especially at night. The methods we use to fall asleep peacefully are good, but we need to remember there are always three angels that guard our sleep.

The first angel is our Higher Power. The second is the positive side of our minds that believes in us. The third is the gentle, hopeful spirit within. Whether we know they are there during the day isn't as important as knowing they are there at night. We are at peace in our sleep because they are there to watch over us.

I know I'm never alone at night. My three angels are watching over me. I'm safe tonight and every night.

Life can only be understood backwards, but it must be lived forwards.

—*Søren Kierkegaard*

One of Mark Twain's most interesting writings states we should live life backwards from the age of eighty to the time we were just a gleam in someone's eye. How much more we'd learn, he felt, if we already knew how to live before we had to.

We may fantasize sometimes about going back with the tools of the program we're using today to our families, our high schools, or our dating years. It may please us to think of how "together" we would be with such tools, knowing what we know now.

But we can't live backwards. Every year we move along in age, experience, maturity, and wisdom. Sometimes we only see such growth on birthdays, when we look back to a year ago at who we were then and who we are now. As our years advance, so do we. Sometimes we need to take a brief look backward in order to see this.

Tonight I'll remember that to see my growth all I have to do is look at where I was a year ago. I have advanced in age, but I've also advanced in wisdom and maturity.

*Our main business is not to see what lies dimly
at a distance, but to do what lies clearly at hand.*
—*Thomas Carlyle*

"Five years down the road," says Jack, "I want to have a new job, an intimate relationship, and a bigger house. I want to be earning more money and feel better about myself." What nice dreams! But what is Jack doing for himself now?

"My relationship is not going well," sighs Sarah. "This isn't the first time I've been told I have the same character defects. Someday I really want to make changes and be in a warm, supportive relationship. Then I'll be happy." But how can Sarah expect to have a wonderful relationship if she doesn't begin her work now?

"My family is so messed up," declares Leslie, a parent. "No one communicates. If we had a bigger house we wouldn't argue so much or be so disorganized. When Bill and I start making good money, we can look for that dream house." But when will Bill and Leslie work on the family problems they're having now?

Tonight I can begin to see what lies clearly at hand—not a dream or goal years away from now. All I have is right now. Tonight I can build my future foundations by working on me.

OCTOBER

I could tell where the lamplighter was by the trail he left behind him.

—Harry Lauder

Before electricity, people were dependent upon lamplighters to light the gas lamps before dark so people could walk about at night in safety. Without light, the streets were dark and ominous—almost impassable.

How many times have we felt as though we were floundering about in the dark, wishing we had a lamplighter to light our way? Many times we may have been afraid to walk alone and became dependent on others to light the way. But they would grow tired. When our dependency became overpowering, we'd look for another lamplighter, and the cycle would repeat itself.

Then we found the program. We've learned we are all lamplighters at one time or another, both for ourselves and for others. Sometimes it may be dark, but we'll soon find another who has traveled that darkened road before. That person will light our way until we can carry our own light. As long as we see ourselves and others as the lamplighters, we will never have to walk alone again.

Help me light someone's path so I won't walk alone.

There seemed to be endless obstacles preventing me from living with my eyes open, but as I gradually followed up clue after clue it seemed that the root cause of them all was fear.
—Joanna Field

How often have we complained that we would be able to do something if only another thing weren't preventing us. "I can't" is our answer when we look around us and see only potential obstacles to accomplishing something. We need to realize, however, that "I can't" is just another way of saying "I fear."

If we took away our fearfulness, think of all we could do. There would be nothing to prevent us from taking risks, trying new things, going new places, becoming more intimate, changing careers, going back to school, taking a Fourth Step inventory, chairing a meeting, or sponsoring a newcomer.

We can change our response of "I can't" to "I'll try." We can take the first step away from our fear toward trying something new. There are no obstacles in our path—only the ones we put there to protect us from things we fear.

Higher Power, help me take the steps to change from "I can't" to "I can."

The nice thing about football is that you have a scoreboard to show how you've done. In other things in life, you don't. At least, not that you can see.

—Chuck Noll

When we entered the program, we learned how much blame we placed on others and how much denial was in our lives. Gradually we began to see our teachers, friends, or coaches weren't against us. As time went on, we learned our bosses weren't against us, or our lovers, or our siblings. In time, we may have even stopped blaming our parents.

We have no scoreboard to measure our progress other than the way we feel. If we feel restless, edgy, anxious, or unhappy, we've got some more work to do, and we can begin that now. If we're content, serene, and peaceful, we need to continue the work we're doing.

Life's ball game is with ourselves. Either we will push on and keep in winning form, or we will ignore our needs and fall behind. It is our choice, for we are the captain and the team.

I can ask my coach—my Higher Power—for help to keep me in winning form. Let it begin with me.

All our actions take their hue from the complexion of the heart, as landscapes their variety from light.

—Francis Bacon

Tests have proven color and light play a significant role in influencing our moods. Even if we don't believe such statements, we can recall how we feel at the onset of a brilliant sunrise or breathtaking sunset. We can remember how we feel after two or three days of gray, overcast skies. The bright and vibrant colors stimulate our senses, and we react to them differently than we react to gray, dark colors.

The colors we wear and the way we decorate our living spaces are pretty accurate reflections of how we feel about life and ourselves. Sometimes dressing in a more brilliant or a softer color can subtly change our mood from sad to happy. Sometimes imagining we are surrounded by a healing color—one of our favorite colors, perhaps—can help lift our spirits. Just as we give a coloring book and crayons to a child, so can we give ourselves a palette of beautiful colors with which to paint ourselves.

I can create a wonder of colors within me and around me. I can color me beautiful!

Know what you want to do, hold the thought firmly, and do every day what should be done, and every sunset will see you that much nearer the goal.

— *Elbert Hubbard*

Every good story has a beginning, a middle, and an end. The beginning is like our morning, full of newness and promise and hope. This morning was our introduction to a new day, to new people, and to new experiences.

The middle of the story is how our day progressed. It's the actions and events, the dialogue and the locales, and the conflicts of the day. The middle may have been dull and boring, or it could have raced along.

The ending of the story is our evening. Tonight we may have found resolutions to the conflicts of the day or logical endings to some of the promises and hopes of the morning. The story's conclusion is decided by how we want to end our day. Why not end today's story with hope, gratitude, and peace—a happy ending!

How will I end today's story? I can write a happy ending with gratitude for the peace my Higher Power has given me.

I guess we are now small enough to go to bed.
—*Theodore Roosevelt,*
To his soldiers, after
gazing at the stars one night

Sometimes after a really "up" day we may feel impervious to troubles and problems. We may even feel a bit cocky if others have depended on us for help and assistance and we've been able to provide what they needed.

It's easy to get off on an ego trip by feeling we're the best when we've solved problem after problem. We may even feel superhuman. But we need to shrink back to our proper size.

Some days are good, and we deserve them. But good days don't prove that we're the greatest or that all our problems are solved. Today we did what we needed to do. We may have had a lot of energy and patience to work with. Tonight we can feel grateful for this positive, constructive energy. But we need to remember we're the same size we were this morning. We're human, not superhuman. Tonight everything is where it belongs. The stars are up in the heavens and we're here looking up at them.

Tonight I can pray for the continued ability to have wonderful days and to feel good about myself.

The great gifts are not got by analysis.
—Ralph Waldo Emerson

Lovers often reflect on how they met and when they first realized they were in love. They'll play back the tapes of courtship as if they were analyzing instant replays of a sports play. "Yes, it was then when we first knew we were in love," concludes one. The other disagrees: "No, I still didn't know you well enough and wasn't ready."

The bottom line is they fell in love. Whether it was Tuesday or April or morning, what is most important is that they did grow to love each other. Not by analysis did they learn this love, but by accepting the gift of love they had for each other.

Analyzing people, places, or things may be a great way to reminisce, but we need to remember analysis isn't as important as what we've received. We aren't given gifts for any reasons. We're given gifts because that's what gifts are for.

Tonight I can stop analyzing why I have a nice family, a good job, supportive friends, or great meetings. I can accept them all for what they are—gifts to be appreciated.

*The turbulent billows of the fretful surface leave
the deep parts of the ocean undisturbed.*
—William James

Picture in your mind a calm lake, its surface like glass reflecting the sky and the full trees along its edge. A short distance from shore a flock of geese float smoothly along the surface. With their long necks extended gracefully, they barely create a ripple on the surface of the lake.

That picture is very serene. But below the surface of the water are a bunch of legs furiously churning. This lake scene teaches us a lesson: things are not always as they appear. A smiling face may not reflect a broken heart. A sleeping child may not reflect nightmares being dreamed. An efficient worker may not reflect the nervous approval-seeker. A responsible adult may not reflect the hurting, angry child within.

Tonight we can think about the appearances we reflect to others. Are we like the smoothly floating geese, not letting anyone see our struggles? Tonight, we can learn that keeping up appearances is really for the birds!

I can let down all appearances and let people see how I really feel. I can be honest and show the emotions that are under my surface.

The ideal day never comes. Today is ideal for him who makes it so.
—Horatio W. Dresser

What kind of day did we have today? Are we critical of the day's events or circumstances because they didn't meet our expectations? Based on our standards of perfection, will we ever have the perfect day?

There is no such thing as a perfect day. Today happened just the way it was supposed to, with its imperfections as well as its achievements. If it was a lousy day, it was only because we believed it was a lousy day. By the same token, today was a good day because we believed it was, not because the sun was shining or traffic was light or we got paid.

Every day is different. Some days may be enjoyable experiences while others may be difficult to get through. But each day plays an important part in our development. Instead of judging each day like a teacher grading papers, we can see each day as our teacher. What we learn from the day, as well as the attitude we have about it, is our daily lesson.

Tonight, can I see today as my teacher? What did I learn today?

I think one must learn a different, less urgent sense of time here, one that depends more on small amounts than big ones.
—Sister Mary Paul

Up until the beginning of our adult lives, our growth depended on big moments: graduation from high school, leaving home, marriage, or entry into the job force. Now that we're adults, we still may have expectations that our lives will be composed of big moments.

But things aren't always so momentous. Job promotions happen over time, as do salary increases. The move from apartment living to ownership of a condominium or house comes after years of saving or years of training for the job with the big salary.

It's important to take our time and savor the smaller moments. Those are the moments we sometimes don't pay attention to because they seem minor and inconsequential when compared to bigger moments. Little moments, like small gift packages, can contain the richest and most satisfying rewards.

What are some of the small but precious moments that happened today? Tonight I can appreciate their rewards, even if they're not the biggest I could get.

People who fly into a rage always make a bad landing.

—Will Rogers

We may have learned rage at a very early age from an alcoholic parent. We may have found we could manipulate people and distance them by taking off at them like a rocket. We found they had no choice but to take cover or speedily undo what they had done to make us angry.

Today, we may feel a need to fly into a rage because we fear someone will see our human, vulnerable side. Now that we're dealing in feelings, our rage may simply be a symptom of our own frustration in the slow process of recovery.

If a mirror were placed in front of us during one of our rages, we probably wouldn't recognize the person in the reflection. We can do far more harm than good, more damage than repair, and generate more feelings of dislike than like. Do we need to fly into a rage anymore? Tonight we can treat raging behavior as a thing of the past and move on to mature, constructive behavior.

Do I remember my last rage? What did it accomplish? Tonight I can work on new scenarios for old, immature behaviors.

If you are too busy to pray, you are too busy.
—*Anonymous*

Our growth depends on our mental, physical, and spiritual health. Yet too often we may spend more time on physical and mental growth than on spiritual growth. When this happens, all three suffer.

Through recovery, we may find we've been able to set aside time for hobbies and relaxation and for eating right and getting enough rest. Yet our spiritual side may be easily sacrificed due to time constraints. A little extra sleep in the morning may mean we have to skip our morning prayer and meditation. A long night of socializing, and our sleepy minds may opt for rest rather than a few moments of prayer.

When we start to cut back or postpone our spiritual times, we're eventually going to harm our mental and physical sides. We need to allow time for prayer and meditation and be able to stick to that time—no matter what!

Do I pray on a regular basis? Tonight let me spend time in prayer and meditation to benefit my mental and physical health.

I could almost dislike the [person] who refuses to plant walnut trees because they do not bear fruit till the second generation. . . .
—Sir Walter Scott

There once was a man who wanted to give up his high-salary job to start a Christmas tree farm. He told his friends about his dream. The first thing they asked him is how much money would he make. "A lot," he said, "once it gets started." "How long will that take?" they wondered. "Years," was his reply. "First I have to purchase the land, then prepare the soil, then plant the seedlings, then tend them with care until they mature. By the time I'm forty-five," he concluded, "I'll have my first Christmas trees to sell."

None of his friends could understand why he would want to take a risk on such a long-term venture. But deep down inside he knew this was his dream and this would make him happy. It didn't matter how long it took for him to get what he wanted. What was important was that he was working on his dream.

Do I have any long-range dreams I believe will never happen because they'll take too long? Tonight I can visualize my dream and take the first step toward making it happen.

There are three things that only God knows: the beginning of things, the cause of things, and the end of things.

—*Welsh proverb*

We learn when we enter the program that we didn't cause our disease, we can't control it, and we can't cure it. Those are the only answers we're given. It's up to us, in our hearts, to place trust and faith that a Power greater than ourselves will take care of the rest of the answers.

Many times we may feel overwhelmed by the disease. We may want to scream at the unfairness of the changes we have to make and at the patience and detachment required of us. We find it's not enough to confront the root of our problems; now we need to look at more than just the problem. But we don't have to do all the work in one night. Tonight we can find relaxation amidst the effects of the disease. There's hope tonight, if we'll only open our hearts to believe that.

Tonight I can trust I don't need to feel overwhelmed by my disease. My Higher Power won't ever give me any more than I can handle.

In the midst of winter, I finally learned there was in me an invincible summer.
—*Albert Camus*

When things seem to be going badly and everyone appears to be against us, what do we see? Do we think things will never get better, or is there a ray of hope inside us that believes everything will soon be okay?

In the midst of a long, cold winter, we might only see the gray skies, feel only the biting chill, hear only the crunch of our feet on the frozen earth. Wintertime can be compared to the bottom we first had to hit before we entered the program—a gray, dreary, hopeless, emotional freeze.

Yet we've learned there is hope. Each day of recovery has warmed the emotional chill and brought new life back into our bodies. We can now trust that even in the darkest and coldest of times, there is a warm glowing ray of hope and faith all around us.

I trust there is hope for even the most hopeless of situations. Tonight I have great faith in the healing of the program.

To make one pound of honey one bee would need to travel 50,000 miles, more than twice the distance around the globe. . . . A single teaspoon of honey in six weeks is a bee's entire life quota.
—Margaret T. Applegarth

A grandmother watched her grandchild open birthday presents. All around the child were toys and records and books that had brought smiles to the child's eyes. But after the child opened the large box and saw what was in it, the smile faded.

"What is it?" the child asked. "It's a quilt made to show the story of your eleven years," the grandmother said. "Here's your very first step and here's the first time you lost a tooth. Here's your first time swimming and here's the birth of your baby brother. Each picture shows you growing and maturing. It has taken me eleven years to make this quilt for you, but you will have that quilt for the rest of your life."

The child is now an adult, but goes to sleep every night under a quilt filled with memories of her early life and the loving patience of her grandmother.

Tonight I need to remember the most special things take time to become special.

We come into this world crying while all around us are smiling. May we so live that we go out of this world smiling while everybody around us is weeping.

—*Persian proverb*

Do we matter to others? Have our lives touched the lives of others? Do we think of ourselves as important and worthwhile?

There are many lives we touch in a day, a week, months, or years. Each of these lives was meant to touch ours. We are meant to exist. We are children of our Higher Power and are watched constantly with love and concern.

We do matter to those around us. Birth, as well as death, heralds the entrance and the exit of a life filled with meaning and purpose. We were meant to be here now, not only for ourselves but for the many lives around us. Our lives are important and worthwhile to all the people we know.

Help me see tonight that my life matters. Just as others have touched me, so have I touched the lives of others.

There is more to life than increasing its speed.
—Mahatma Gandhi

We live in an age of instant coffee, one-minute managers, and same-day mail delivery. The speed of living seems to increase every year with improved methods of communication, travel, and manufacturing. Because of this we may feel our daily work in the program and the subtle changes in our behavior are not fast enough. How can we keep pace with the world if we're spending years on recovery?

It is the quality of a thing that is important. Instant coffee is a great convenience, but brewed coffee tastes better. Driving in the fast lane all the way to a destination will get us there faster, but we won't enjoy much of the scenery we pass through.

Life isn't a race won by the fastest. If we set a goal and don't attain it within the time frame we set, we do not fail, we readjust our schedule. Living to the fullest doesn't mean living in the fast lane. It means taking the scenic route, stopping often to appreciate the view, and sharing the ride.

I can slow down my pace and appreciate the road I travel by taking my time and meeting fellow travelers.

Lo! in the middle of the wood,
The folded leaf is wooed from out
*   the bud. . . .*
With winds upon the branch,
*   and there*
Grows green and broad,
*   and takes no care.*
                                    —Alfred, Lord Tennyson

What does it take for us to be drawn out of ourselves? So many of us have retreated inwardly and are
afraid to open up in social situations. We may refuse
invitations to gatherings, may be afraid to meet new
people, and may want to remain in uncomfortable but
stable situations.

When a plant grows a new leaf, we see evidence of
a shoot. Then we see the leaf grow longer, curled tight
like a cigar. Finally, with nourishment and safety, it begins to unfurl. This leaf supports new life, and the
healthy plant grows.

We, too, are like that new leaf. As we grow, we learn
there are environments where we can open up and be
safe. It's okay to close up when there are people or situations around us that are unhealthy. But we need not
fear everybody or everything. We can be safe. We can
proudly unfurl ourselves for all to see.

Am I withdrawn because of fear? Tonight I can find a safe
person, place, or thing and open myself up in safety.

*Happiness grows in our own firesides and is not
to be picked in strangers' gardens.*
                                    —Douglas Jerrold

The old saying "The grass is always greener on the
other side of the fence" is an appropriate sentiment for
envious people. When we look at another couple or
another family, we may only see the good points. We
may look for the same good points in our relationships and families and not find them. We then con-
clude our happiness, security, and contentment can
only occur if we have what others have.

In an old comedy routine, a restaurant customer
points to another diner and says to the waiter, "I'll
have what she's having." The waiter immediately takes
the half-eaten food from the other diner and gives it to
him. However, we can't take the good things that others have, nor can we share them. We can only learn
from them, making things better in our relationships
and families. Only we can make things good.

*Have I been envious of other people and what they have?
Tonight I can discover what good I'd like to have in my life.
Then I can take steps to bring this good from within me.*

Life is made up of sobs, sniffles, and smiles, with sniffles predominating.

—O. Henry

The balance in life places us between happiness and sadness. Life can't always be ecstatically happy and free from woe, just as it isn't always miserably unhappy. Somewhere in the middle is a gray area where neither smiles nor sobs predominate.

Living life on its terms means accepting the events life brings without overreacting with ecstacy or depression. Acceptance sometimes means we may not feel happy and we may not feel sad—we may just feel. This is the middle ground of feeling that isn't high or low—it seems indefinable.

We don't always have to feel great. Sometimes we can just feel okay. Accepting that middle-of-the-road feeling and not trying to analyze it or define it gives us the freedom to have gray areas in our lives. And sometimes it is the gray area that keeps us from bouncing off walls or riding an emotional roller coaster. Accepting the gray area can give us sanity.

Tonight I can find the gray area in my life and realize not everything has to be good or bad—sometimes it can just be.

Every year I live I am more convinced that the waste of life lies in the love we have not given, the powers we have not used, the selfish prudence that will miss nothing, and which, shirking pain, misses happiness as well.
—Mary Cholomondeley

When we were children our teachers or parents would talk about realizing our full potential. "He's a bright child," they might have said, "but he's not working up to his full potential." What is our full potential? And how do we realize it?

We all have certain abilities. With these we can learn, play, love, mature, take risks, make decisions, and speak our minds. Before the program, we may not have developed abilities to do some of these things.

When we avoid developing an ability, we are not realizing our full potential. If we don't learn to play, we lose social skills and the fun-oriented part of us. If we don't work on our capacity to love, we lose emotional and spiritual growth. By growing to our full potential, we can live life as whole people.

I can begin to include those long-ignored areas and take the first step to becoming a complete and whole person.

I do not know what I appear to the world, but to myself I seem to have been only . . . playing on the seashore . . . whilst the great ocean of truth lay all undiscovered before me.
—Sir Isaac Newton

Before the program we chose to see only what we wanted and turned away from any distractions. We may have been aware of obsessive or addictive problems, but those were off to our left or right. We may have seen the emotional or physical breakdown of a person or family, but this was also off to the side. What lay ahead was just getting through a day and on to a future we hoped would be better.

The program has helped us deal with the problems we always put off. Today we know we must meet every problem face-to-face without running away or avoiding it. What lies ahead of us is no longer as important as what lies right in front of us.

Are there issues I've been avoiding? Tonight I can take one of those issues and see it clearly. I will be unafraid to meet the challenge.

A hug is a perfect gift—one size fits all, and nobody minds if you exchange it.

—Ivern Ball

In the past many of us may have feared physical expressions of friendship. A hug, a touch, or a friend's gentle nudge may have made us want to back away. Or we may have misinterpreted such expressions as overtures to more physical contact. All we knew is that those hugs or touches were confusing.

When we came into the program we saw many people hugging or holding hands in the circle at the end of a meeting. We may even remember the first time someone hugged us; their arms encircled us as our arms lay stiff by our sides. "What can this person possibly mean by hugging me?" we may have thought.

As time went on and we received more hugs, we realized they didn't hurt. It didn't mean someone wanted us sexually; it just meant somebody liked us and wanted to show us that. Pretty soon we started giving hugs instead of just receiving them. We learned to trust them and soon let ourselves feel the wonderful love that encircled us each time we were given one.

I can give a hug to someone I care about. Maybe I can get a hug too!

Our weak and negative states leave us open to 'take on' outside prevailing conditions. . . . We are shaken with the wind and float with the current because we present the negative.
—Henry Wood

A bad day usually begins badly. All it takes sometimes is one thing to go wrong and we run to our battle stations for the rest of the day. Then it seems all that ever comes our way are more bad things. By the end of the day, we're glad it's over.

But our day didn't have to go badly if only we had detached right from the start. Instead of believing we were victims of an unset alarm clock, a ripped shirt, unpressed pants, an angry partner, demanding children, or burnt toast, we could have accepted the upsets and let go of them.

Life is so much better when we aren't drowning in the upsets around us. We don't have to absorb the antics of others or get caught up in the material and mechanical inconveniences. A sure sign of maturity is being able to accept an upset for a few minutes and then let it go.

Tonight, I can let go of minor hassles and upsets and enjoy what lies ahead tomorrow.

When nothing seems to help, I go and look at a stonecutter hammering away at his rock perhaps a hundred times without as much as a crack showing in it. Yet at the hundred and first blow it will split in two, and I know it was not that blow that did it—but all that had gone before.

—Jacob Riis

Many times we may hear at a meeting that the length of time in the program isn't as important as the quality of the work we do. Someone with five years of recovery isn't necessarily healthier than someone with three years of recovery.

No one accomplishes everything within a mere amount of time. The greatest achievements are the results of accumulated experience, maturity, and the application of healthy principles.

Today is just a brief entry in our daily journals of recovery. What we do tonight may not draw all the loose ends of our lives together, but may tighten one or two a little more. Tomorrow holds great promise for us if we can see it as another page in our lives instead of as the whole book.

Higher Power, help me forget my destination and remember instead the joy of journeying toward that place.

I observe myself and so I come to know others.
—*Lao-tzu*

If we could view a film of ourselves at the end of the day, we would see ourselves as others see us. We would notice our facial expressions and tone of voice and body language. We would be able to see our actions and reactions. We could study ourselves closely and learn so much more.

How wonderful it would be if we could take an equally close view of those around us! Think of how much we could learn about those close to us if only we paid attention to their facial expressions, their tone of voice, and their body language. We would get to know them and understand them so much sooner if we only paid attention to them the way we sometimes pay attention to ourselves.

If we observe ourselves, we will be able to understand the same actions and reactions in others. The mirror we place before ourselves is but a reflection of those around us.

Can I take the time tonight to observe my actions? How can I use such insight to learn about other people?

Tears may linger at nightfall, but joy comes in the morning. Carefree as I was, I had said, 'I can never be shaken.' But, Lord, it was Thy will to shake my mountain refuge. . . .

—from Psalm 30

A great force has shaken us from our caves of isolation. We may have first felt this force at our first meeting. Somehow, we knew we had made the right choice. We belonged.

We next felt this force during a time of incredible need and fear. We may have wanted to run to the farthest reaches of our caves, but once again we felt something telling us to stay vulnerable and remain exposed. We may then have fallen to our knees or simply closed our eyes and silently asked for help.

Our prayers have been answered. Today we know we always have that cave to run into, but we seem to need it less. The great force that shook us from our refuge also gave us refuge. Tonight—as always—we are safe and secure as we stand exposed to the world.

There is a great force in my life who has saved me from isolation, desolation, and despair. I feel wonderful because of this!

Call on God, but row away from the rocks.
                                    —*Indian proverb*

Wouldn't it be foolish if we sat in our room tonight and moaned about how dark it is? All we would have to do is reach over and turn on the light. Yet aren't there times when we call on God to help us when we can really help ourselves?

Establishing a conscious contact with our Higher Power doesn't mean we're going to build a dependency on this Power. This Being doesn't exist for us to make request after request for things we can do ourselves. It's okay to ask for God's safety and guidance in the midst of difficult situations, but it's up to us to take the initiative for our own safety and well-being.

Whenever we need guidance, safety, security, peace, and strength, we can certainly call on our Higher Power. But let's make sure we take responsibility when it's needed. God works through us, not *for* us.

What can I take responsibility for in my life tonight? Help me help myself.

One cannot step twice in the same river, for fresh waters are forever flowing around us.
—Heraclitus

Do we sometimes feel bored with our lives? Do we feel like we're doing the same things, following the same schedules, working to get out of the same rut we've been trying to change for a long time? Do we wish to make changes, but don't know where to start?

Imagine living in front of a wide, picturesque river. In the living room of the house is a spacious window that allows a magnificent view of the river. Every day we might see this same scene and believe it is never-changing. But in reality, it is ever-changing.

Each day we see with new eyes. And each day nature astounds us with newness and growth. That water we're watching flow by today isn't the same water we saw yesterday. A stick thrown into the water yesterday is far downstream today. We can see this river in two ways: stagnant or flowing. So too can we see our lives.

Tonight I can look at my life as if it were a river, always changing as it flows.

There are always two voices sounding in our ears—the voice of fear and the voice of confidence. One is the clamor of the senses, the other is the whispering of the higher self.
—*Charles B. Newcomb*

Sometimes we may wish others could hear the station our heads are tuned to. When someone says, "You look nice," our station says, "They're only saying that to get a ride to town." When someone says, "You're fun to be with," our station broadcasts, "If they only knew what a bummer you really are."

The host of our station is Fear; his assistants are Doubt and Insecurity. The trio is always on our airwaves, ready to shoot down any good vibrations we receive. If we start to believe we are good people, then we'll put them out of business.

We can let a new voice onto the airwaves—Trust. When we hear, "You look nice," Trust can say, "You've been trying to improve your appearance and someone noticed!" If we learn to listen to Trust, we will hear affirmations and motivating statements. With Trust we will always hear the Truth.

———

Tonight, I will believe I am a much better person than Fear, Doubt, and Insecurity would have me believe.

NOVEMBER

When it gets dark enough, you can see the stars.
—*Lee Salk*

The tiny points of light in the darkened sky have long been used to plot navigational courses. In fact, sailors trust the stars even more than their most sophisticated instruments. We, too, can look at the sky and find reassurance in its light.

Each star in the sky has meaning. Whether it's part of a major constellation or merely a pulsating, burning mass in the sky, there is a reason for that star to be there.

We are also stars in the night. We are not alone, for we share the expansive heavens with those around us, whether our nearest neighbor is one floor above us or miles away. We are all here for a purpose.

I know I am not alone tonight, for I can see the stars.

Our daily thoughts should be elevated above the ceiling.

—W. W. Loflin

How optimistic are we? Do we see problems as solvable or impossible? Do we see our abilities as expanding or limited? Do we set goals for ourselves, or do we feel goals are unattainable?

Not everyone can scale the highest mountain or find the *Titanic* or survive great disasters. We can't all be president of the country or director of our department. But elevating our daily thoughts above the ceiling doesn't mean we have to strive for recognition or undertake the most difficult tasks. All we really have to do is believe we are good people, capable of enjoying health and happiness. That belief can buoy us up against any obstacle.

We can learn to raise our thoughts whenever they start to go down. First, we can say we are inherently good. Then we can show others our goodness by being kind, friendly, and helpful. Finally, we can ask that our spirits be kept high by the help of our Higher Power. By doing these things, there is no limit to how good we can feel.

I can learn to raise my thoughts when they start to go down.

*Do what you can, with what you have, where
you are.*
— *Theodore Roosevelt*

Suppose we were walking down a street when
someone came over to us and said, "I want you for our
Olympic volleyball team." We may protest, saying we
haven't had the training or haven't developed the
skills or even allowed time for this to happen.

Yet we may treat the program as a different kind of
example. We may jump right in and expect we'll grasp
all the Steps and slogans, suddenly have a marvelous
relationship with our Higher Power, and be ready to
sponsor every fledgling that walks through the door.

We can't join the Olympics today, and we certainly
can't expect to master the work of the program today
either. Each takes a great deal of time to develop the
necessary skills. Each requires a dedication and perseverance that strengthen us as we grow stronger and
more confident. Each requires us to feel like we're part
of a team, which can't happen unless we meet all the
members of the team and work with them. Tonight
we're doing the best we can, with what we have, right
where we are in recovery.

---

*Tonight I can participate as a member of an active
recovery team, but I'm not ready yet to be the most
valuable player. I need more time to work with myself and
the team.*

Free will is not the liberty to do whatever one likes, but the power of doing whatever one sees ought to be done, even in the very face of otherwise overwhelming impulse.
—George MacDonald

There are certain things we cannot do, whether they are restricted by law, are moral issues, or are safety concerns. We may know this now, but in the past this fact may have meant little to us. We may have driven drunk, beaten partners, or verbally or sexually abused our children.

Free will doesn't mean we can do anything we please. Free will means doing things like changing bad tempers, drinking habits, or unacceptable behaviors. With free will, we have the choice to make changes, even though they may be difficult.

Nothing is impossible if it is within our control. We can use free will to opt for change and improvement. With free will, we can choose when and how we will change. If we choose, we can begin tonight.

Are there changes or improvements I can make in my life? Help me know I'm free to change these things whenever I'm ready.

One never notices what has been done; one can only see what remains to be done.
—Marie Curie

Here's a familiar scene: Several people have come to our homes ready to sit down to a turkey dinner with all the fixings. In the kitchen is a dirty oven, messy pots and pans, cluttered counters. Which do we think about—the wonderful dinner we have prepared for family and friends or the kitchen?

Many times we notice what has to be done, not what has already been done. When we first came into the program, we learned we had so much to do: detaching, admitting, accepting, working the Steps, working on ourselves. We may have felt overwhelmed at what needed to be done, but old-timers may have pointed out what we already had done—we came to the program to find help.

Tonight, are we thinking about tomorrow or a week from now? There are many things left for us to do. But for right now, we can look at what we have accomplished in our lives, our careers, our families. We have done so much, if we can only recognize it.

Tonight I can give myself credit for all the growth and gains. I have done well!

Constant togetherness is fine—but only for Siamese twins.

—Victoria Billings

Fusion in relationships can be self-destructive. Bonding so tightly with one person, with little time spent apart, is a perfect setup to addiction. When we become addicted to a person, we can be as desperate and suffering as an addict without a fix.

Growing up, we may have spent hours fantasizing about how wonderful relationships were. We may have placed so much hope in dreams of a perfect relationship that once we met someone, we unconsciously smothered the other person and ourselves in togetherness. We may have believed time spent apart meant our partner didn't love us or care to be with us.

Each flower in a garden has a separate set of roots, separate stems, leaves, and buds. Although the flowers may be the same variety, each is different in a subtle way. Similarly, we grow with our partner, like two separate flowers sharing the same garden. Our roots may intertwine and our leaves touch, yet we still grow and flourish separately from the other.

Tonight I can spend time flourishing on my own, relaxing for a peaceful night's sleep.

And if you but listen in the stillness of the night
you shall hear. ... It is Thy urge in us that
would turn our nights, which are Thine, into
days, which are Thine also.

—Kahlil Gibran

How much would we benefit from the program if
we went to meetings with cotton stuffed in our ears?
We could use the Steps and read the literature, but
how would we learn from others about the strength,
hope, and experience of the program?

Listen and Learn may be one of the hardest slogans
for us to follow. Many times we come to meetings
ready to dump our problems on the group. Sometimes
we sit in judgment of those around us. Each of us, no
matter what our background or age, shares a com-
monality. Each of us has something important to
share, whether the words be delivered eloquently or
with humor, sadness, or simplicity.

We can pause before we speak to listen to others. By
opening our ears, we are opening our minds to learn
about ourselves through the words of others.

Can I listen to those around me? What can I learn that
might help me?

The best prayers have often more groans than words.

—*John Bunyan*

Sometimes we may find it difficult to put into words the thought we'd like to send to our Higher Power. After a day filled with a wide array of emotions, we may find it difficult to summarize in our evening prayers words that will convey our deepest thoughts and innermost reflections.

Rather than attempt to find the words, we can use actions and thoughts to communicate. Our prayers can be filled with visualizations of how we'd like things to be. Our prayers can be a time to cry or yell.

However we're feeling tonight, there's no set of rules for prayer form. We don't have to say, "Higher Power, I'm in pain." We can cry and just as easily and clearly communicate hurt and pain. Unlike people, our Higher Power is a mind reader who always knows how we feel and what we need.

Tonight I don't have to struggle to find the right words for my prayers. How I feel is my best prayer.

I had the blues because I had no shoes, until upon the street I met a man who had no feet.
—*Harold Abbott*

A young man traveled to the city to apply for jobs. But first he wanted to buy new shoes to assure a good impression. He was so intent on getting to a shoe store that he nearly tripped over another man. This man had no legs and was sitting on a board with wheels, pushing his way along the sidewalk when the two had bumped. But the accident in no way slowed down the disabled man; he waved a cheery greeting to the young man and traveled on.

How often are we so caught up in petty trifles that we don't notice others? The young man so concerned with shoes and a future job learned some people don't have to worry about shoes.

What did we notice today? If we think back to to-day's events, can we remember little details about people, recall smiles and laughter, or recollect snatches of conversation? We can take time to notice more than our shoes.

Sometimes I pay too much attention to my own issues. Help me notice other people and remember the time I spend with them.

Life consists of opposites in balance.
— Marian Zimmer Bradley

Remember playing on a seesaw and trying to achieve the balance that meant we and our friends could sit on opposite ends of the board, suspended in the air without the board moving up or down? To achieve such a balance we had to have only one thing in common with our friend: similar body weight.

Tonight we're still on that seesaw. We've spent our day trying to balance all that came our way. Some things may have weighed us down; others may have buoyed us in the air. Through living each day, we've learned that neither the high nor the low stays around long enough to tip the balance too far.

No matter what sits down on the opposite end of our board of life, we need to remember achieving balance is the important thing. When we are balanced, it means we have equalized both the good and the bad with our strength, hope, faith, and security.

The center of the board of life never moves. Help me to keep this center within me tonight.

A satisfied flower is one whose petals are about to fall. The most beautiful rose is one hardly more than a bud wherein the pangs and ecstacies of desire are working for larger and finer growth.

—Carl Sandburg

Every one of us in the program is a flower in a beautiful garden. The ones who move down the road of recovery are blooming right and strong. The newcomer and short-timers are just buds, soon to open in a burst of energy and color.

Our Higher Power tends this garden and provides us with room to grow, rich soil in which to root, ample nourishment, and the company of others. We are not all alike in this garden. We each bloom a different color, have a different petal pattern, and release our own fragrance. Yet our sensuous mixture yields an amazing scene of color, fragrance, and life.

At times we may feel uncomfortable in the garden. We may not feel as wise as some of the older flowers and may think our newness is still too bright. Yet we all belong and we will all be nourished as long as we are within the garden walls.

Do I believe I am unique and beautiful? I will let myself be part of the uniqueness and beauty in the program.

How vastly different a troubled question looks to us at noonday and at midnight. We flinch in the hours of darkness from a problem we can meet bravely when we are on our feet, and under the momentum of the noonday vigor.
—*Charles B. Newcomb*

We've often heard the phrase, "Things will look better in the morning." Somehow in the light of day, in the hustle and bustle of routines, our problems seem to recede from the shores of our minds. But as the hours turn from day to night, shadows lengthen, the stream of life stills, and our problems seem ready to wash up once again at our doors.

Perhaps we trust the day more because of the light and nature's rhythm. As night the darkness shrouds our vision, nature stops its movement, and people seem to be on their own rhythms. Yet we can trust the night by depending upon the light of the program and the natural flow extolled by the slogans. We can create our own rhythm and clear vision to see our way through a problem. Tonight can be secure to us if we will only trust.

I can work out solutions to my problems tonight as easily as if I were in the light of day by using the tools of the program.

The glory of friendship is not the outstretched hand, nor the kindly smile, nor the joy of companionship; it is the spiritual inspiration that comes to one when [one] discovers that someone else believes in [one]. . . .
—*Ralph Waldo Emerson*

Many times we may not totally believe in ourselves. After a bad day or a painful rejection, it may be hard for us to look at ourselves and say, "But I believe in you."

Yet there are people who can tell us that. In our lives we need to have at least one special friend who has a belief in us even when we don't. Sometimes just to hear a friend say, "It's going to be all right. I believe in you," is enough to help us get back on track with our self-esteem.

A friend can be many things: a confidante, a buddy, a good-time pal. In all of these roles, a friend confirms one solid fact: a belief in our goodness as a person. The measure of any person is not by the number of friends, but by the belief any one friend has in that person.

Who is it who believes in my goodness as a person? Tonight I can give thanks for this friend and his or her belief in me.

Some minds remain open long enough for truth not only to enter but to pass on through by way of a ready exit without pausing anywhere along the route.

—*Sister Elizabeth Kenny*

Many times what someone says hurts us. If someone is pointing out a character defect or being critical of our work, we may find it difficult to listen. But before we react, we need to ask whether the person is being destructive or constructive in his or her speech. We can ignore destructive words by detaching, but we need to listen to constructive words. There is a reason to hear such words, even though they may hurt or make us feel defensive.

To become a total listener rather than a selective listener, we can let people finish what they need to say. Silence and an open mind can help us hear all their words. By truly listening and then responding maturely, we will grasp the message and perhaps see the love and caring with which it is delivered.

Tomorrow, I will not react to things said to me. I will truly listen and then respond maturely and gently.

*Delegate freely . . . and check on it every chance
you get.*
—*Linda Johnson Rice*

When we ask that something be done, do we let go
and let the job get done, or do we worry it won't be
done on time or how we want it? Part of learning to
trust others is to learn when to let go and let other
people handle something in their own way.

We can look back on today and remember requests
we made. Perhaps we asked an employee for assistance, a child to do a project, or our partner to do
something important. After we made the request, did
we then let go or were we filled with worry and doubt
about whether our request would be honored?

Tonight we can let go of our requests and trust all
will be taken care of. If it is not, that doesn't mean we
can never trust anyone again. It may mean our request
was unreasonable or other circumstances intervened.
It's okay if we make a request and don't get results that
meet our expectations. Trust doesn't mean we will get
what we want when we want it and how we want it.
Trust means having enough faith to ask another—and
to let it go.

Tonight I can let go of requests unhonored today.

What, after all, is a halo? It's only one more thing to keep clean.

—*Christopher Fry*

Those of us who continually strive for perfection may find we place incredible demands upon ourselves. One minute we're working toward serenity, and the next we're busy every night of the week. One minute we say we're going to sit down to read, and the next we're up cleaning the house, rushing from room to room in nervous energy.

Perfection places an incredible demand upon us to do everything right. But what is right? Is there a right way to do something and a wrong way?

The perfectionist in us is always looking for right, but we'll never find it. There really is no right way or wrong way to do anything. It's whatever way we choose. If we choose to try wearing the halo of perfection, we need to know it can be tarnished, tipped to the side, or misplaced every once in a while.

I'm no angel, that's for sure, because I'm not perfect. I'm still working on my halo and wings, and that's a lifelong process.

*It is universally admitted that there is a natural
healing power resident in the body. . . . Many
people have learned to relax and to keep quiet
like the animals, giving nature a free
opportunity to heal their maladies.*
—Horatio W. Dresser

Have we ever met people who never seem to get
sick? They eat well, get plenty of rest and exercise, and
generally seem to give physical health a priority. Then
there are those who always seem sick, and they seem
more concerned about their sickness than in getting
better.

Medical studies have found a direct correlation between people's emotional and physical states. The person who thinks positive thoughts and expresses
emotions usually spends less time being sick than
someone who has a mind filled with stinking thinking.

We are our own healers. Our minds and bodies tell
us when to eat, sleep, and relax. When we listen, we
are in touch with the ways we can help ourselves feel
better. It's our choice—we can feel healthy or we can
feel sick. Which will it be?

*Tonight I can learn to listen to my body and respect its
messages. I will take care of myself and get the rest I need.*

The past is our cradle, not our prison. . . . The past is for inspiration, not imitation; for continuation, not repetition.

—Israel Zangwill

A history book informs us about the past. It gives us an objective picture of what life was like during particular time periods. With such a view, we can then see how far we've come. How do we apply our own histories to our present lives?

We can learn much from our past. It may tell us about some uninspiring things and some negative experiences. But it can also give us clues about our present behaviors, personalities, and mood swings. It can tell us about our dreams and desires, gifts and goals, talents and tastes.

We can use our past as a springboard for our present way of living. We can look away from the negatives of the past and choose not to imitate or perpetuate such negativity. We can then reflect upon the good parts of our past and use them to inspire our present work.

How can I use the good parts of my history for my best benefit?

Never accuse others to excuse yourself.
—Anonymous

How many times have we blamed our feelings at the end of a day on the boss, co-workers, teachers, parents, or even the person who cut us off on the road? It's true we may feel anger or resentment toward any one of those people, but they didn't cause our feelings.

We are the sole owners of our feelings. We're the ones who bought them, and we're the ones who will hold on to them. When we're ready to let go of them, that's when we won't feel them any longer.

There are no excuses we can use to justify our feelings. The program teaches us to look inward at ourselves, not outward at the effects of the universe. Tonight we can look inward and survey the feelings we have. We can choose to keep them, or let them go.

No matter what the circumstances of the day, all the feelings I have are mine. Tonight I can let go of the ones I don't want and hang on to those that feel good.

Life: a diary in which every [one] means to write one story, and writes another.
                                        —*Sir James M. Barrie*

Did our day today live up to our expectations, or were we greeted by new situations, new knowledge, and new experiences? Oftentimes what we expect is not what we're given. Life is not a known substance. It's many times a delicious new taste we've never had before.

To go through each day with a set outcome in our minds will only lead to disappointment and may prevent us from being open to new discoveries. Life cannot be predicted or even imagined. It can only be experienced each minute.

Let us not try to write the events of tomorrow until after they've happened. Let us be free to experience all that's in store for us—fresh and new and exciting.

What will I write in my diary? Let me meet each new experience of life on its own terms.

The first three times you came with the same story [they] would listen and try to help. But if you showed up a fourth time and it was the same old tired things, the others in the circle would just get up and move. . . . It was time you did something about it.

—Anne Cameron

Many of us go to meeting after meeting, talking about the same problem. What are we looking for? What are we asking for? We aren't asking for help, because we usually are given good suggestions that we reject. We aren't looking to make changes, because we keep holding on to the same problem.

We may also have been in the opposite position— listening to one who keeps talking about the same problems. After hearing those people for a while, it's easy to want to tune them out.

But we can change. We can ask whether we use meetings to air the same grievances. If so, we need to stop complaining and do something. If we hear another doing the same thing, we can learn from that person's unwillingness to change. We can learn the difference between stagnation and growth.

I can listen and learn. If I ask for help, let me also be willing to accept it.

No answer is also an answer.

—Danish proverb

Have we ever prayed and felt God must not have heard us because our prayers weren't answered? We may have asked for strength or protection or for things to change. Yet hours, days—even weeks—later we may still be in the same situation, feeling the same way.

God always hears us, but sometimes the answers aren't immediate or guaranteed. Sometimes the best answer is no answer, meaning we need to stay in an uncomfortable situation a little longer. Perhaps there is something we need to learn that can't be learned unless we find it on our own.

We aren't abandoned when our prayers are answered by silence. Silence teaches us to listen closer, observe longer, and learn more in order to find our answers.

Is there anything tonight that confuses me or makes me feel helpless? I can find my answers by remaining open to all the messages I'm given.

I can't write a book commensurate with Shakespeare, but I can write a book by me.
— *Sir Walter Raleigh*

We may have grown up trying to emulate our favorite heroes, wishing we were as strong, as beautiful, as smart, or as self-sufficient as they were. Because our role models in the home may have been poor, we learned to look outside ourselves for people to copy.

Yet we can never be anyone other than ourselves. We may desire to have what someone else has because we don't like what we have. We can change those characteristics we don't like in ourselves, or we can learn to accept them. But we can't disguise our true selves by trying to be the carbon copy of someone we admire.

By striving for imitation, we are ignoring the wonderful person inside. We may not be a great artist like Renoir, a celebrated writer like Shakespeare, a brilliant singer or actor or great athlete or superb politician. We can only be ourselves. And that means we need to write our own book, not copy another's.

Tonight I am proud to be who I am. I have some wonderful qualities and talents that I can develop.

A great obstacle to happiness is to expect too much happiness.

—*Fontenelle*

How happy is happy? When we're laughing and joking, are we happy? Or is happiness doing an activity we really enjoy? Perhaps happiness is a feeling we get when we see a beautiful sight or a happy child.

Who knows what happiness really is? Like love, happiness can't really be defined, for what is true for one person isn't for another. Happiness really comes from within. If we feel a sense of contentment, peace, or joy, then we can bet we're feeling some form of happiness.

As long as we're satisfied with that happy feeling, then we'll feel happiness. It's when we expect happiness to feel differently that we'll lose our happy feelings. To be happy, we need to feel the happiness that exists, even if it isn't the way we've fantasized it to be.

Have I felt happiness today? Help me reflect on the feelings of that happiness and to allow myself to feel similar feelings.

You might as well live.

—Dorothy Parker

Many times we may have thought of quitting this life. We may have experienced close friends or a relative who chose such an end. But suicide isn't a resolution, it's a stop in midsentence. Running away from any pain, whether it be by suicide, drinking or using, or denial, may make distance—but not decisions.

Every life has its hard times, its pitfalls. To feel pain or go through hard times doesn't mean we've got to be hermits. It means we need to seek comfort, compassion, understanding.

When one person in the program is in pain, there are hundreds of others ready to guide that person to peace and serenity. We can let ourselves be guided by those around us.

Tonight, I can remember I am not the only person who has ever felt pain.

Never answer an angry word in kind. It's the second word that makes the quarrel.

—*Anonymous*

In the past we've probably found it's easy to have an argument. In fact, that may have been how we spent the majority of our time with our spouse, family members, or friends. Arguments may have become so familiar that to have them was to be doing "the right thing."

Today we've learned to detach from angry words. We know now the other person is probably in so much pain that the only way they feel they can alleviate the pain is to hurt another.

Detachment is the only cure for an argument. Once we stop detaching, we are sucked into the tangled web of confusion, pain, and bitterness. We can strengthen our ability to detach by relying on the support of our friends in the program and our Higher Power.

Do I need help detaching? Help me find my strength from those who can help me, not hurt me.

Failure is an event, not a person.
　　　　　　　　　—*William D. Brown*

We may find it easy to blame disappointing circumstances in our lives on the people in our lives. We might think we wouldn't be so angry with ourselves if we could change bosses or co-workers or partners. We might believe our inability to stay in relationships is caused by the family that brought us up or the circumstances now in our lives.

If we're angry at one boss, chances are we'll be angry at another no matter what company or job we have. The co-workers at a new company can't guarantee our happiness or peace of mind any more than a new relationship will bring us the love we've always searched for.

Once we realize our dissatisfactions come from events, rather than people, we'll be less likely to place blame on people or make them the targets of all our failings.

I can stop trying to discover shortcuts or easy answers to why I feel dissatisfied at times. I am the only one who can make changes, right here and now.

Selfishness always aims at creating around it an absolute uniformity of type. Unselfishness recognizes infinite variety of type as a delightful thing, accepts it, acquiesces in it, enjoys it.
—Oscar Wilde

If we think of those who take care of themselves as selfish, we need to look at our definition of selfish. If we want to stay up late and talk and another person doesn't, who is selfish? The person who is tired and wants to sleep, or the one who insists he or she stay up?

Stating a limitation is not selfish; we are taking care of our needs and being honest. Selfishness is when we insist we have our way at the expense of another's needs. Selfishness is dishonest, because it doesn't honor the truth expressed by another.

To be unselfish, we first must be able to listen to others. After we learn to listen, we need to accept what is expressed. And to be truly unselfish, we must be able to enjoy the difference in others. When we can delight in the variety of people around us, we have achieved true unselfishness.

Can I accept the differences in others? I can begin by listening to others and learning just how different we all are.

The most important thing in life is not to capitalize on your gains. Any fool can do that. The really important thing is to profit from your losses.

—William Bolitho

It is easy to see the profit in what we gain, but it is not so easy to see the profit in what we lose. Projects that take shape and collections that expand show the gains we have made. But how can we see profits from the end of a relationship, the loss of a job, or the estrangement from family?

Each loss represents a step we need to take toward maturity and growth. Throughout our lifetimes we will walk up many steps. Sometimes it may seem like we have a never-ending stairway in front of us. Our gains are the level parts of each stair, but the real progress is made when we climb the stairs of our losses.

Although we may feel as though we have nothing when we go through a loss, what we do have is the experience of the loss. We learn to deal with a different lesson. Our profits from a loss may not show up immediately, but we will discover the rich rewards as we learn to accept life on its terms—not on ours.

Tonight I can learn to look at today's losses as gains. What have I learned? How have I grown?

*Simply to live is a wonderful privilege in itself.
. . . But to what are you alive? Is it merely to a
daily routine? . . . How much do you really live
outside of your chosen profession or occupation?*
—Henry Wood

From an acorn to a tree, the oak puts all its energy
into growing as strong and tall as it can. Moisture,
sunlight, and nutrition are gathered for its leaves,
acorns, branches, and trunk. Yet if our oak tree takes
all the moisture, sunshine, and nutrition, other nearby
trees will be weaker and smaller.

We have within us a forest that demands attention
for its growth: a career tree, a family tree, a recovery
tree, a parent tree, and a friendship tree. If we spend
more time and attention on one than the others, the
neglected ones will not grow strong.

Every part of our lives should be important to us:
our families and friends as well as our recoveries and
careers. It may be commendable to receive lots of promotions at work. But if our families are neglected, the
forest inside us will not flourish. Every part of life
needs attention for us to succeed.

*Tonight I can begin to balance my time. All areas of my life
need attention.*

DECEMBER

The woods are lovely, dark, and deep,
But I have promises to keep,
And miles to go before I sleep,
And miles to go before I sleep.
—Robert Frost

We made a promise to ourselves when we joined the program—to use the tools of the program, *One Day at a Time,* to stay on the road to recovery.

We need to remember that promise every day. Our program needs come first. After a long day at work or school, it is tempting to turn on the television or take a nap. Instead of calling someone we sponsor or our own sponsor, we may not feel like talking. We may come up with many excuses not to go to a meeting, like doing laundry or balancing the checkbook.

But all these things can wait while we take care of *First Things First.* It may take a lot of energy to stay alert in a meeting, but we'll be doing the best thing we can for ourselves: keeping our promise. Let's keep that promise, beginning tonight with prayer and meditation.

Have I spent time using my program today? What can I do to keep my promise to myself?

There is no royal road to anything. One thing at a time, all things in succession. That which grows fast withers as rapidly; that which grows slowly endures.

—Josiah Gilbert Holland

During winter we can walk through a grocery store and see an array of fresh vegetables and fruits as if it were summer. Chemicals and greenhouses allow farmers to grow food year-round and produce ripe tomatoes even while a snowstorm howls outside.

Yet the tomato that took a few weeks to grow in a climate-controlled, enriched environment doesn't compare to the one that grew to fruition over months in the natural sun and soil. So it is with us. Instant recovery is like instant breakfast—it's satisfying but doesn't last long.

Many times our recovery will seem like it's proceeding at a snail's pace. But emotional growth can't be regulated like temperatures and soil conditions. Our potential for growth is a result of the effort we put into it and the time we give it. The steady regulation of time forces growth to be gradual and balanced. For growth to be good, it must stand the test of time.

I can slow down my desires and not try to push time to move more quickly. I need to accept the pace and grow steadily and surely.

The [person] who is always having . . . feelings hurt is about as pleasant a companion as a pebble in a shoe.

—Elbert Hubbard

Are we overly sensitive or afraid of personal criticism for fear our feelings will be hurt? Sometimes it may seem like no one can say anything to us without us feeling hurt, shameful, guilt-ridden, or rejected. We may find ourselves saying we're sorry so many times in one day that we end up believing we are, indeed, very sorry people.

Our friends and relatives care about us and want to see us healthier, happier people. Because of this, they may give us criticism. This criticism is meant to be helpful, not hurtful.

If we feel attacked by the criticisms of others or always seem to have our feelings hurt, it's because we allow it. No one can make us feel any way unless we let it happen. Although we may have been brought up with criticism and been told we were no good, the only person today who can make us feel worthless is ourselves. We are as good as we'll allow ourselves to be.

I can accept personal criticism and not fear my feelings will be hurt. Tonight and every night, I am a good person, no matter what another says or feels.

They got scared when they started feeling good, just because it was so unfamiliar. Like chronic prisoners facing release from their cells.
—Lisa Alther

The evening news usually begins with doom-and-gloom stories and perhaps ends with one positive, uplifting item. If we were to give the evening news of today, what would it consist of? Stories of disappointment, anger, resentment, and misunderstandings; or recollections of giving, laughter, closeness, success, and achievement?

It's scary to focus only on the good things that happen. Many times we're afraid to feel good because we don't trust the feeling to last long. Perhaps we're very uncomfortable with good feelings because they're so unfamiliar. Yet that unfamiliarity can change, over time, until we grow accustomed to the good.

Accepting good feelings is like meeting someone we really want to know better. At first we may feel scared or shy. But in time, we feel more at ease and relaxed as we spend more time together and share different things. Feeling good can be a friend that will grow more important to us every day.

Tonight I will focus on the good in my evening news.

Character builds slowly, but it can be torn down with incredible swiftness.
                                    —*Faith Baldwin*

Because we are fragile and sensitive, we may feel like our progress is more steps backward than forward. We can take pride in our gains, but losses have a way of throwing us into a tailspin.

We may be progressing nicely in recovery, when one person says, "I don't like what you're doing." Suddenly our self-image changes from that of hope and faith to depression and despair. We become uncertain and confused about where we're going and what we're doing. How much do we value that person's opinion?

Before we let one person break our fragile self-esteem, we need to remember that person's opinion is only one of many. We need to trust our own opinion. Then we need to trust the guidance and support of people familiar with the program and do the character building we wish to do. Then we will find ourselves taking more steps forward and fewer backward.

Tonight I need to remember some people who mean a lot to me but who will never understand or support my new life. I can still care for them, but I don't need to seek their approval.

We either make ourselves miserable, or we make ourselves strong. The amount of work is the same.

—Carlos Castaneda

"Woe is me!" is a familiar cry to many of us, for we have cried it ourselves long and hard. We've placed a lot of energy into feeling our misery, in discussing it, in analyzing it, in living and reliving it. Misery has been our favorite tape recording, to be played over and over.

But our awakening in the program has taught us that we do not have to live in misery. We are learning we have choices, and one of those choices is to hold on to our feelings. If we choose to hold on to pain and despair and misery with both hands, we have no way to grasp on to strength and hope and happiness.

We can let go of misery tonight. Perhaps we won't want to release both hands right away, and that's okay. But we can release the grip of one hand and have it grasp on to positive, strength-giving feelings. Little by little, we'll learn to let go of our misery and use both hands to hold on to the hope of the program to make ourselves strong.

I do not need to fear letting go, for nothing bad will happen to me—only good.

When you get into a tight place and everything goes against you till it seems as though you could not hold on a minute longer, never give up then, for that is just the place and time that the tide will turn.

—Harriet Beecher Stowe

After every downswing there is an upswing. It may not be immediate, like a roller coaster ride with its constant dips and climbs. Sometimes there will be a long stretch of level ground after a downswing, making us feel we are sinking lower and lower. But the leveling off period strives to bring us stability before the upswing.

Listen to those around us. They will talk of bad times and say, "I never thought it would come to an end." But they'll also tell us the end did come and things did get better. Each time that happened they had more faith and the next downswing wasn't as devastating or hopeless. By trusting in the natural up-and-down motion of life, we will be able to say, "Things won't get any worse. In fact, they will get better."

I need to listen to others with experience and trust their stories. Tonight I will believe and trust as they do.

A strong life is like that of a ship of war which has its own place in the fleet and can share in its strength and discipline, but can also go forth alone to the solitude of the infinite sea.
—P. G. Hamerton

We need to achieve a balance between socializing and solitude. If we are around others day in and day out, we will never learn what it feels like to be by ourselves. Likewise, if we are isolated a lot, we will never learn what it's like to be around others. Recovery depends on sound balance between the two.

As we reflect upon today, we can take note of the time we spent with others or in solitude. Then we can better decide how to balance tomorrow's activities. If we've dealt with people all day, it might be good to spend some time alone, traveling in solitude on the infinite sea. If we've spent most of the day in solitude, it might be good to spend time with others, experiencing that we are a part of those around us. We can strive to seek balance and harmony as we steer our ships.

What do I need to balance tomorrow's activities: the company of others or the company of myself?

Risk! Risk anything! . . . Do the hardest thing on earth for you. Act for yourself. Face the truth.
—*Katherine Mansfield*

Many times when we feel fear we don't realize it's related to a risk that we have the option to take. A risk doesn't have to be as dramatic as climbing a mountain or placing all our money on a bet. A risk can be walking into a new meeting, smiling at a familiar face, or purchasing our first program literature.

In the beginning, we may feel fear taking small risks. As time goes on, we learn there is nothing to fear at a new meeting, at smiling at another, or reading literature that tells us who we are. Then we begin to take greater risks, like asking someone to be our sponsor, going out for coffee, or taking the Fourth Step.

The safety and security we feel when we take risks in the program will help us take risks outside the program. With time, we can learn to trust others, share our needs, and set our limits at home, at work, and with friends. Taking a new risk allows another to soon appear.

What is there to fear in taking a risk? Help me learn that each time I take a risk I open another door.

Actually, these are among the most important times in one's life, when one is alone. Certain springs are tapped only when we are alone. The artist knows he must be alone to create; the writer, to work out his thoughts; the musician, to compose; the saint, to pray.
—Anne Morrow Lindbergh

Most of us are alone for some time at night, whether we're commuting home or sitting down for a few minutes of meditation. Time alone—with ourselves and our Higher Power—is a valuable part of our day. In this stillness, we can listen to ourselves and feel our feelings without the constant distractions of the day.

Being still with ourselves means not running away from the silence around us. It means feeling our feelings, whether they're good or bad. It's a time of reflection and prayer.

For every moment we can be at peace with ourselves, we are that much closer to being a part of life. For as there is peace in nature, so it is in our nature to feel peace.

Am I at peace with myself now? Have I prayed to my Higher Power to help me at this time?

You cannot be anything if you want to be everything.

—*Solomon Schechter*

Sometimes we may feel overwhelmed by the amount of things we believe we have to work on at one time. We may feel stressed under the pressure of working a full-time job, attending school, working on a relationship, caring for ourselves and a family, and growing in recovery. Sometimes we may want to put up an "Out to Lunch" sign and take off for parts unknown.

Anytime we feel overwhelmed it's our mind's way of telling us we need to set limits. We can't do everything and expect to get very far. But we'll get far if we do some things and leave others alone for a while.

Tonight we can look at our overbooked schedules and see where we can make changes. We first need to leave some free time for ourselves. Then we need to prioritize our obligations. Once we try out our new schedules for a while, we may see some changes or find others that need to be made. Starting tonight, we can stop feeling overwhelmed with life and take charge of it.

How can I reorganize my schedule so I'm not so overwhelmed? Tonight I can begin to take charge of my life and mold it to fit my needs.

The reputation of a thousand years may be determined by the conduct of one hour.
—*Japanese proverb*

For the next hour, how will we act or feel? Will we toss and turn filled with fear and worry over the night? Will we be anxious and stressed over our day's activities and unable to sleep? Will we feel lonely and abandoned in our isolation? Or will we be able to sleep peacefully?

If we let this next hour determine how we would feel for the rest of our lives, which feelings would we choose? We might find it easy to let go of the negative feelings we feel right now if we knew we'd have to feel that way all the time.

For the next hour, we can choose how we want to feel just as if we were making a permanent character mold. Chances are we want a good night's sleep, so we can face the new day relaxed and filled with good feelings. Then we can approach the day an hour at a time, maintaining those positive feelings. Imagine what good we can feel if we look at our lives as a series of hours that can be changed and improved as each one is completed!

For the next hour, I would like to relax and begin a peaceful night's sleep. Then I can face tomorrow in a positive mood.

We cannot build until we have laid foundation stones. We add to our foundations every time we meet our difficulties well, however insignificant they may be.

—Charles B. Newcomb

A house without a foundation will not last. As the ground shifts in hot and cold weather, so will the floors. The wood placed upon the ground will rot. The rooms will be cold and damp with no protection from the temperature of the ground. Before the program, we were houses without foundations.

A house built with a strong foundation will provide warmth in the winter and coolness in the summer. Though the ground may shift, the foundation will absorb the movements and keep the rooms level and unharmed. The foundation will protect the precious wood. In the program, we are houses with foundations.

The strength of our foundations will depend on our commitment to recovery. If we keep the program ever in our lives, work the Steps, and take regular inventory of our progress, our foundations will be strong and durable. They will protect our houses through all kinds of weather for a long time.

Tonight I can make repairs upon my foundation and strengthen it.

In the old days, if a person missed the stagecoach he was content to wait a day or two for the next one. Nowadays, we feel frustrated if we miss one section of a revolving door.

—Modern Maturity

Many things today can take place overnight. We can cook a turkey dinner, mail a package several states away, or travel to another continent in a matter of hours. Because the world moves at such a fast pace, it's only natural that we absorb some of that frenetic activity into our own lives.

We become accustomed to wanting change to happen right away. When we share that at a meeting others may laugh, but it's because they, too, have had the same feelings. It's not unusual to want miracles with the blink of an eye.

But just because the outer world is at a frantic pace doesn't mean we, too, have to operate at such a pace. When all the world is a raging stream, we can have a small peaceful stream of serenity flowing within us.

Tonight I can learn patience that things will happen in my time, not the time of the world. Everyone moves at his or her own pace, and I need to move at mine.

When you pray for God's guidance, don't complain when it is different from your preference.

—Our Daily Bread

When we were children we sat on Santa's lap with our lists, or asked the tooth fairy for more money, or begged the Easter Bunny for more candy, or prayed to God for that shiny red bike we wanted. Yet we usually ended up with things we didn't even ask for, but needed, like warm jackets and winter boots or pajamas.

Today we may still pray to God for things we want. Maybe not shiny red bikes, but shiny new cars, more money, better jobs, greater security, or the health of loved ones. Our prayers might not be answered in the way we'd like them to be. We may never win a lottery, we may lose a promotion, or we may experience the death of a loved one.

Yet what we are given is what God feels we need. Though we may be sad or disappointed, those things help us grow in the way we need. Sometimes we may get just what we pray for, and that's wonderful. But if we don't get what we ask for, we must remember that what we get is the gift God feels we need.

I can pray for guidance without any expectations. I know I will get what I need.

Some days confidence shrinks to the size of a pea, and the backbone feels like a feather. We want to be somewhere else, and don't know where—want to be someone else and don't know who.

—Jean Hersey

Who are we? Where are we going? What do we like? Are we happy? What do we want from life?

These certainly are not easy questions to answer. In fact, we may have been struggling with the answers for a long time. We, who thought we knew ourselves so well, are now finding we aren't who we believed we were. We are so much more, but we may not be able to put our finger on the so much more.

We may never get to answer all the questions. For some of us, the answers may change on a daily or even hourly basis. We are just starting to learn who we are without the definitions of people, alcohol or other drugs, or any other addiction. The process of finding out who we are takes time and patience and a whole lot of change from the way we used to be. The answers, like the questions, will come to us when we're ready.

I am just starting to discover who I am. I may not have all the answers tonight, but I know so much more than I did before.

We crucify ourselves between two thieves: regret for yesterday and fear of tomorrow.
                                                    —*Fulton Oursler*

Some women who had been victims of violence banded together to "take back the night" in a series of public demonstrations. Rather than hold regret over the violence or their fear of what might happen, they chose to live in the moment with no fear or regrets.

Tonight we can "take back the night" from our own fears. This can mean easing our minds from the stress of the day so we can have a peaceful sleep. It can mean letting go of any fearful thoughts so we're at peace in our homes. It can mean blocking out crazy thoughts that will make us toss and turn.

This night is ours. It's our time for uninterrupted sleep, pleasant dreams, and gentle rest for our weary bodies.

Tomorrow will be waiting for me, after I've taken back the night to feel peace, trust, and serenity.

The preservation of health is a duty. Few seem conscious that there is such a thing as physical morality.

—Herbert Spencer

Do we realize we have an obligation to our bodies to stay healthy? Before we entered the program, we may have abused ourselves with chemicals, diets or binges, little sleep, or chains of cigarettes and coffee. Now that we're in the program, we're beginning to realize our mental health has a direct bearing on how we treat ourselves physically.

If we've been cooped up in an office or home, we need to pay attention to getting fresh air and exercise. We can go for a walk, meditate, or take a warm bath. We can eat a nutritious dinner and get to bed early for a good night's sleep. Just as we have a moral obligation to our mental health, so too do we have a moral obligation to our physical health.

I can eat good foods, breathe in fresh air, and exercise for my best benefit. Tonight I will rest soundly to treat my physical health well.

What is the source of our first suffering? It is in the fact that we hesitated to speak. It was born in the moments when we accumulated silent things within us.

—Gaston Bachelard

We may have learned while growing up that it was easier not to communicate. We may have remained silent rather than risk an argument or a reprimand or a misunderstanding. But as adults, we need to unlearn that behavior and learn to give voice to the muted feelings, thoughts, ideas, and grievances within us.

We first need to risk breaking silence, for the silences we hold within us are like cancers. For as long as we ignore them, they will continue to grow and we will suffer. But if we strive to remove them—one at a time—we will become cleansed of their ill effects.

We may discover things we wanted to say, but didn't. We can prevent these silences from growing by taking positive action. There are those who will listen to us—our Higher Power, a trusted friend, a meeting group. But it is up to us to take the first step.

Now is the time to give voice to our inner silences.

'Tis pitiful the things by which we are rich or poor—a matter of coins, coats and carpets, a little more or less stone, wood or paint, the fashion of a cloak or hat. . . .
—Ralph Waldo Emerson

What are riches? Are they the luxurious feel of a mink coat, the weight of a bulging wallet, a filled jewelry box, or the size of a bank account or stock portfolio? Or are riches intangibles—things we cannot see or touch or earn or spend? Perhaps riches are happiness, serenity, and faith.

Recalling Dickens's tale *A Christmas Carol*, we remember that even with all the riches imaginable, Ebenezer Scrooge was miserable and friendless. The happiest and most contented man was Bob Cratchit, who was poor in wealth, had a crippled son and other children to feed and keep healthy. Yet his home and his heart were filled with love, peace, and faith.

We can ask our Higher Power for the greatest riches: peace and joy in our hearts and homes. We don't need presents or luxurious finery to make us happy. To become richer, we need to open our hearts to the wealth of wonderful feelings around us.

Tonight, let me give thanks for the riches I have inside. Those are the greatest gifts I can receive from my Higher Power.

It usually happened ... particularly at the beginning of a holiday. Then, when I was hoping for nothing but sleep and peace, the chattering echoes of recent concerns would race through my head, and the more I sought rest the more I could not find it.

—Joanna Field

Stress, anxiety, fear, and worry are especially dominant before holidays. The upcoming family events, gift exchange, cooking, and scheduling seem to take precedence. Yet there are ways to find peace and serenity amidst all the excitement.

Instead of focusing on things we don't like about the upcoming holiday season, we can focus on things we do like. Such things may be as simple as: "I'm looking forward to seeing my sister," or "I like receiving cards from old friends," or "I like the snow on the pine trees."

We can have a nice time this season by putting energy into the things we enjoy. We can go to many meetings, make plans with close friends or our sponsor, and meditate to keep calm and serene. Tonight we can put the stress of the upcoming holidays to rest by remembering ourselves first.

How can I use the program to relax my thoughts tonight?

*. . . I finally figured out the only reason to be
alive is to enjoy it.*

—*Rita Mae Brown*

We've probably made many changes in our lives
since we joined the program. We may have improved
our job performance. We may be attending school,
struggling to attain the degree we never got when we
were using. We may be spending a majority of our
evenings at meetings instead of partying as we did in
the past. And we may feel life isn't fun anymore—that
it just doesn't have the excitement of the past. But did
we *enjoy* our lives before the program?

Today we're learning to live in a whole new way. We
made a lot of changes in our behavior. And we're
learning to enjoy things we never did before—to appreciate a beautiful sunset, to look forward to being
around people at a meeting.

If we forget to enjoy today's precious moments, we
can change that right now. Tomorrow is full of enjoyment yet to come!

*Have I enjoyed my life today? What can I do to enjoy my
life tomorrow?*

People disturb us. They sap our vitality from us. ... They pile upon us their conditions of fear and their atmosphere of despondency. In such cases we must regain our poise by the realization of the power that is ever within us. Find your center.

—Horatio W. Dresser

Did we become wrapped up in the behaviors of other people today? If we haven't detached from the problems of our boss, co-worker, or family member, we feel drained and used—like an old rag that's choked with years of dust and dirt.

Other people own their behaviors just as we own ours. If we buy into someone's attitude, then we have purchased a piece of that attitude. It's ours to feel, and feel it we usually do. Suddenly we become a reflection of the other person, displaying whatever emotions he or she is experiencing.

Now that the daytime is over, we can reflect upon our feelings and ask if they are ours or ones we purchased from others. To find our center, we need to discover the feelings that are ours alone. As we interact with people, we can refuse to purchase any more attitudes that are not our own.

I can detach from others and not buy their feelings. Tonight I will find much serenity from my own feelings.

If time be of all things most precious, wasting time must be the greatest prodigality, since lost time is never found again.
—*Benjamin Franklin*

At the beginning of a day we may feel we have so much time ahead of us. But now as we look back on the day, we may feel we never had enough time to do all the things we wanted. Here we are now, ready to say good night to the day, and not satisfied that we did all we wanted to or could do.

Perhaps the day didn't go as we had planned. Perhaps the list of things we wanted to accomplish barely got touched. Perhaps we feel we wasted a great deal of time watching television, shopping, or talking on the telephone.

If we believe now we wasted time today, then we'll view that time as useless. But if we view all of the moments of today as precious and necessary, then we won't feel so critical of how we spent our time. We did what we wanted to do today, in the time we were given. Tonight we can rest—assured—that none of our time was wasted.

I'm satisfied all of my time today was valuable and useful, even if I didn't accomplish everything I set out to do.

When you feel grateful for something others have done for you, why not tell them about it?
—Anonymous

It's one thing to express gratitude for the many wonderful things in our lives, whether we do so in our prayers or to our group. But to go one step further and express gratitude directly to the people who help us feel grateful is one of the best ways to show love and kindness.

Our direct contacts with others don't always need to be in making amends. Recognition of the gifts we receive builds a strong bridge that can continually transport positive, loving feelings.

We can enlarge the one-way avenue toward us into a two-lane road that returns to the ones who show us so much patience, kindness, and love. Once we do, we'll find we want to travel this road often, both to receive and to give thanks for what we receive.

Is there someone to whom I can express my gratitude? I need to take time for a prayer of gratitude for the wonderful gifts I have received.

Without prayer, I should have been a lunatic long ago.

—*Mahatma Gandhi*

How can we make our prayers more satisfying and fulfilling? One of the best ways is to see and hear ourselves as we pray, as if we were getting a bird's-eye view of what we look like and how we sound when we pray.

Seeing from above in this objective way gives a good overview of the strength and the meaning of our prayers. Are we whining and fidgeting as we pray? Maybe we aren't really praying but instead are asking to get our way. Do we sound angry, with fists clenched? Maybe we need to work on letting go first before we pray.

This is how our Higher Power sees and hears us. Our Higher Power know which prayers are serious, meaningful conversations and which are filled with self-pity, resentment, and anger. Tonight we can hear ourselves pray and learn whether we are truly praying or merely taking time for self-centered feelings.

Before I pray tonight, let me run through the things I want to say. Help me keep self-centered feelings at a minimum and true sharing and communication at a maximum.

Life is like playing a violin solo in public and learning the instrument as one goes on.
—*Edward Bulwer-Lytton*

The violin virtuoso whose concerts are sold-out has spent innumerable hours of practice to achieve such fame. That person wouldn't think of inviting the public to a practice session because of the flaws they might hear.

We aren't virtuosos, yet we're always on view to the public. Everyone gets to see our good performances as well as our bad. Because of this, we may often struggle with impatience and disappointment in our striving to "look good" in front of others.

Yet we're all struggling in front of one another. Just as others see our imperfections, so do we see theirs. None of us are virtuosos in life. To become skilled in living, we need to live *One Day at a Time* and learn as we go.

I don't need to strive for perfection and skill. I can just be myself in front of people.

One does not have to believe everything one hears.

— *Cicero*

As we were growing up, we may have been told many things about ourselves. Some may have been complimentary, but others may have been vicious and degrading statements made by a chemically dependent parent or guardian. Because we were caught in the disease, we may have believed all the horrible things that were said.

But today we don't have to buy into anyone's negative comments. We don't have to believe we are no good, we're stupid, lazy, helpless, insecure, inept, or will never amount to anything. Anytime we believe those messages, we're allowing a label to be stuck to our chests.

We can choose to walk around advertising our labels, or we can take them off and rip them up. We can turn away physically and emotionally from the source of the negative comments. The only label we should wear should say we are good people.

Tonight I can affirm I'm a good person and that I deserve the best.

It is important for every one who is trying personally to apply these principles, to understand that all progress is vibratory and uneven. The higher standpoint is only reached through a long series of 'ups and downs.'
—Henry Wood

Are we expecting some magical signal to occur when we're "cured" of the symptoms of our disease? Do we believe once we "master" the tools of the program we won't feel pain, sadness, resentment, or disappointment? Are we still anticipating a happily-ever-after to occur in our lives?

Life is naturally full of ups and downs. Every day isn't all sunshine and perfect temperatures. Nature has its tragedies and destruction as well as its growth and harvest. If we see both good and bad as complements to each other, we will see life is a continuous process.

If we apply the principles of the program, our lives will get better. The ups and downs won't go away, but we will stop focusing on only one or the other. We will see it all as part of the same picture.

My only expectation tonight is to let life flow the way it's meant to.

I wish you the courage to be warm when the world would prefer you to be cool.
—*Robert A. Ward*

For years we listened to the demands of the world and tried to meet them. We may have listened to our parents and did what they told us to do. We may have heard the needs of a lover or friend and tried to meet them all. We may have even paid heed to absolute strangers, making changes in ourselves to honor their opinions.

Like a reptile, we may have absorbed the temperature of our surroundings and adjusted our body temperature accordingly. We may have found comfort in being warm when the world was warm or being cool when the world was cool.

But tonight we can, in the words of Thoreau, march to a beat of a different drummer. We can say no when others want to hear yes. We can set limits when others ask too much. We can even be warm when the world wants us to be cool. Others don't have power over us anymore. Only we have power over ourselves.

Tonight I won't let anyone or anything have power over the way I feel. I can feel warm or cool—it's my choice.

Ring out, wild bells, to the wild sky,
The flying cloud, the frosty light:
The year is dying in the night;
Ring out, wild bells, and let him die.
—Alfred, Lord Tennyson

Past New Year's Eves may have meant times of excessive chemical use. We may have embarrassed ourselves in many ways. We may have chosen New Year's Eve as a time to analyze our past behaviors and write long lists of how that was going to change.

Yet tonight is like any other night. We don't have to feel as though we aren't having a good time unless we're at a party or a bar. We can celebrate the new year tomorrow with those closest to us by doing something we enjoy. The past is gone, the future has not arrived. The present is all we have, here and now.

Look to ourselves and what we want to do, not at what we think we should be doing. We can share our feelings at a meeting, spend quality time with our families and loved ones. We need to focus on ourselves and what we need to do for us, and not be diverted by the craziness around us.

Tonight is an ending; tonight is a beginning. Help me stay in the moment to bid farewell to the old and welcome in the new in my own way.

INDEX

A

ACCEPTANCE . . . . .July 10, Aug. 24, Sept. 8,
Sept. 26, Nov. 3, Nov. 28

ACHIEVEMENT. . . . . .Feb. 5, March 16, April 3,
June 30, Nov. 5

ACTION. . . . . .June 24

ANGER. . . . . .April 29, June 28, Sept. 25,
Oct. 11

ANXIETY . . . . .Jan. 6

APPRECIATION. . . . . .March 17, Aug. 12, Oct. 18,
Dec. 22

ATTITUDE. . . . . .May 23, June 13, July 11,
Aug. 22, Oct. 20

B

BALANCE . . . . .Jan. 29, March 23, May 5,
Oct. 21, Nov. 10, Nov. 30,
Dec. 8, Dec. 29

BEAUTY . . . . .July 24

BEGINNING . . . . .Jan. 3, Feb. 3, June 1

BEHAVIOR . . . . .May 28

C

CARING. . . . . .Jan. 20, May 26, Oct. 24

CHANGE . . . . .Jan. 2, March 7, April 16,
June 4, July 23, Aug. 3,
Aug. 21, Aug. 26, Sept. 18,
Oct. 2, Oct. 30, Nov. 21,
Dec. 11

CHARACTER. . . . . Feb. 19, July 22, Aug. 10,
                                    Sept. 22, Nov. 27, Dec. 12
CHOICES. . . . . May 16, June 26, July 18,
                                    Aug. 5, Dec. 30
COMMUNICATION . . . . March 2, May 2, July 4
CONFIDENCE . . . . Aug. 8, Oct. 19
CONNECTEDNESS. . . . . Feb. 28, April 20
CONSCIENCE . . . . March 28
CONTROL. . . . . Jan. 16, April 5
COURAGE. . . . . Feb. 17, April 6, April 11,
                                    Sept. 15
CREATIVITY . . . . Jan. 27
CRITICISM . . . . Dec. 3

D

DETACHMENT . . . . Nov. 26
DISCIPLINE. . . . . Jan. 25, May 18
DREAMS. . . . . March 1, May 8, Oct. 13

E

EMOTIONS. . . . . April 24
ENTHUSIASM. . . . . Jan. 17
EXPERIENCE . . . . May 27

F

FAILURE . . . . June 27
FAITH. . . . . Jan. 8, Feb. 21, July 2,
                                    Sept. 14
FEAR. Jan. 12, March 8, May 21,
                                    June 5, Aug. 9, Oct. 1

FEELINGS ....Feb. 16, April 14, May 4,
June 10, July 17, Aug. 4,
Sept. 16, Nov. 19, Dec. 23

FLEXIBILITY...............June 18, Sept. 1

FORGIVENESS.............March 3, Sept. 27

FRIENDSHIP...............March 10, July 19, Aug. 6

G

GIFTS ....March 5, Oct. 7, Dec. 20

GOALS ....Jan. 26, March 26, Oct. 5

GOD'S PLAN..............Jan. 14, April 25, July 13,
Nov. 1, Dec. 15

GRATITUDE ....Feb. 18, April 8, June 29,
July 16, Aug. 7, Dec. 25

GRIEF.....................Sept. 13

GROWTH ....April 1, May 7, June 25,
July 26, Aug. 13, Sept. 6,
Sept. 29, Dec. 2

GUIDANCE...............Jan. 23

H

HABITS....................May 24

HAPPINESS...............Jan. 4, March 9, May 19,
Aug. 31, Nov. 24

HATE ....Aug. 19

HEALING.................April 23, June 8, July 20

HEALTH..................Jan. 13, Feb. 29, Nov. 17,
Dec. 18

HELPING.................Feb. 11

HIGHER POWER..........Jan. 21, Feb. 6, March 20,
May 31, July 25, Sept. 2

HOLIDAYS................Dec. 21

HONESTY ....Feb. 7, Aug. 20, Oct. 8

HOPE ....April 15, May 6, June 20,
                        Dec. 7

HUMANNESS.............June 2, Oct. 6

HUMAN RIGHTS..........May 22

I

INDEPENDENCE..........Sept. 23, Nov. 6

INTERDEPENDENCE.......July 3

J

JOY ....March 15

JUDGMENT..............Jan. 10

K

KINDNESS................April 12, Sept. 9

L

LAUGHTER...............Aug. 15

LEARNING ....Feb. 9, Oct. 27, Nov. 7,
                       Nov. 29

LETTING GO ....Feb. 4, March 29, May 10,
                       Oct. 25, Nov. 15, Dec. 6

LISTENING...............Jan. 24, May 17, Aug. 11,
                       Nov. 14

LIVING FULLY............May 29, Aug. 29, Oct. 23

LIVING IN THE MOMENT..Feb. 12, March 12, April 17,
                       May 13, July 6, Sept. 30,
                       Oct. 10, Nov. 18, Dec. 31

LONELINESS ....Sept. 4, Sept. 28

LOVE .... Feb. 14, May 12, June 16,
Sept. 7, Sept. 12

M

MAKING AMENDS .... April 4
MEMORY .... Jan. 5
MISTAKES .... Feb. 24, July 30, Sept. 17

N

NEGATIVITY .... Jan. 30

O

OBSTACLES .... March 22
OPENNESS .... Feb. 15
OPPORTUNITY .... May 14
OPTIMISM .... April 27, July 15, July 21,
Oct. 15, Nov. 2, Dec. 4

P

PAIN .... March 13, April 10, Nov. 25
PARENTS .... Jan. 18, May 11, June 14
PATIENCE .... March 25, July 5, Aug. 27,
Sept. 10, Oct. 16, Dec. 14
PEACE .... March 21, June 3, Aug. 17,
Dec. 10
PERFECTIONISM .... May 20, Oct. 9, Nov. 16,
Dec. 27
PERSEVERANCE .... Jan. 15, July 27, Oct. 26
POSITIVE THINKING ..... July 1, Sept. 11
POWER .... June 6

PRAYER .... Jan. 7, Feb. 22, April 21,
Sept. 20, Oct. 12, Nov. 8,
Dec. 26

PRINCIPLES .... March 18

PROBLEMS .... March 31, May 30, Nov. 12

PROCRASTINATION ...... Jan. 19

PROGRESS................ Jan. 11, April 22, May 25,
June 19, July 7, Oct. 3,
Dec. 5

PROMISES .... Dec. 1

R

REACHING OUT .... March 19, Nov. 9

RECOVERY .... Aug. 18, Sept. 21, Dec. 13

REFUSAL SKILLS.......... March 27

RELATIONSHIPS........... Feb. 25, April 19, Aug. 1,
Oct. 17

RELAXATION.... .... Jan. 1, Feb. 23, April 9,
May 1, June 17, July 8,
Aug. 25, Sept. 5

RESPONSIBILITY.......... July 14, Oct. 29, Nov. 4

RISK TAKING.............. Feb. 2, Dec. 9

S

SECURITY .... March 30

SELF-AWARENESS .... Feb. 26, May 15, July 9,
Oct. 4, Dec. 16

SELF-CENTERED.......... June 22

SELF-ESTEEM............. Jan. 22, Feb. 13, July 28,
Aug. 14, Nov. 13

SELF-IMAGE..............March 6, April 13, July 29,
Sept. 3, Nov. 23, Dec. 28

SELF-PITY ....June 7

SERENITY ....July 31, Aug. 16, Aug. 28,
Oct. 14, Dec. 17

SHARING.................Jan. 31, April 26, Aug. 30

SILENCE ....April 2, Dec. 19

SOLITUDE................Feb. 8, June 11

SPIRITUALITY ....Jan. 9, Sept. 19, Oct. 28,
Nov. 22

SPIRITUAL STRENGTH.....March 14

STRENGTH...............Feb. 10, Feb. 20

SUCCESS ....Aug. 23

T

TALENTS ....April 30, June 12

TIME....................April 28, Dec. 24

TODAY ....Nov. 20

TRUST...................Feb. 27, March 24, May 9,
Oct. 31

TRUTH ....Jan. 28, July 12

TWELVE STEPS ....April 7, June 23

U

UNDERSTANDING.........Feb. 1

UNIQUENESS.............June 21, Nov. 11

W

WHOLENESS ....March 11, Oct. 22

WISDOM ....March 4

WISHES ....June 15

Other titles that will interest you .

Today's Gift
Daily Meditations for Families

Today's Gift is our first daily meditation book written with the family in mind. A collection of readings written specifically to help us, as individuals, deal with our family concerns. *Today's Gift* is an excellent companion for those of us involved in A.A., Al-Anon, Alateen, Adult Children of Alcoholics, and other self-help groups. *Today's Gift* will inspire discussion among family members—child and adult alike—and help us all to pause, regain a sense of balance, and recognize the riches we have within and around us. 400 pp.
Order No. 1031

The Promise of a New Day
by Karen Casey and Martha Vanceburg

Written in the tradition of *Each Day a New Beginning*, this guide reaches out to all people who seek full, healthy living. One page at a time, one day at a time, these mediations will guide your path, affirm your strength, and give you hope and peace. *The Promise of a New Day* is a fine meditation book for men and women looking for greater rewards in daily life. 400 pp.
Order No. 1045

For price and order information, or a free catalog, please call our Telephone Representatives.

HAZELDEN

1-800-328-0098
(Toll Free. U.S.,
Canada, and the
Virgin Islands)

1-651-213-4000
(Outside the U.S.
and Canada)

1-651-257-1331
(24-Hour FAX)

http://www.hazelden.org
(World Wide Web site on Internet)

Pleasant Valley Road • P.O. Box 176 • Center City, MN 55012-0176